Preparing Fields

for

Seasons of Change

Rebecca Collison

Trilogy Christian Publishers

A Wholly Owned Subsidiary of Trinity Broadcasting Network

2442 Michelle Drive

Tustin, CA 92780

For information, address Trilogy Christian Publishing

Rights Department, 2442 Michelle Drive, Tustin, Ca 92780.

For information about special discounts for bulk purchases, please contact Trilogy Christian Publishing.

Manufactured in the United States of America

10 9 8 7 6 5 4 3 2 1

Library of Congress Cataloging-in-Publication Data is available.

ISBN 978-1-64773-166-3

ISBN 978-1-64773-167-0 (ebook)

This book is dedicated to the memory of Mimi and Pop, for the rich layer they added to the soil of my life and the seeds they planted that continue to bear fruit in generations beyond themselves

With God's power working in us, God can do much, much more than anything we can ask or imagine. To him be glory in the church and in Christ Jesus for all time, forever and ever. Amen. Ephesians 3:20-21 NCV

FOREWORD

The primary challenge for most small churches is self-worth. How do you assert your value in a competitive religious market where larger congregations offer better locations, better facilities, better worship with paid musicians, better specialized ministries, better everything? Those of us who care about the small church summon the tools of the Bible, ecclesiology, history, group dynamics, narrative philosophy, and psychology to argue their native worth. Rebecca Collison summons another tool: the immediate agricultural setting of many local churches.

Collison writes from her own setting in southern Delaware where forty-two percent of the land is still farmland, with most of it in the two southernmost counties. Her images are drawn from that location with its flat land, moderate climate, and long growing seasons. Her use of images (soil, labor, seasons, crops) invites the reader to find parallels in their own setting whether it is South Dakota, Virginia, or Pennsylvania. She further invites us to flip our view of that rural agriculture setting as an obstacle to be overcome (a project of modernity) over to a perennial source of vitality and meaning.

Collison's message to the many local congregations located in rural agricultural settings is simple: don't overlook your location! Listen and learn from the land!

"Through the lens of the land, the human story of faith unfolds and informs the church today, specifically the small rural church that finds itself close to the land in agricultural regions".

Collison offers us a new (but actually very old) cache of analogies and metaphors for the Christian faith in general and the small rural church in particular. She mines for us the agricultural images of the Bible, from the garden of Genesis to the fields of Ruth, from the timeless parables of Jesus to Paul's careful parsing of itinerant ministry (1 Corinthians 3:6). And she mines the close-at-hand agricultural experiences of those who are gathered in and sent out from local congregations.

The heart of the book is the comparison of the life of the congregation with the four basic movements of farming, the *fallow, planting, growing,* and *harvest* seasons. The reader will find themselves nodding in agreement at the wisdom offered under the final three headings: the pulling up and turning over of *planting*, the waiting and trusting of *growing,* the hustle and extravagance of *harvest*.

But I believe the first movement, the *fallow* season, will resonate most strongly with persons in small churches today. The fallow season "when fields are bare and nothing seems to be growing" certainly describes many small churches with their empty pews, lack of activity, the absence of apparent growth, poor communication, and financial need. But things are happening beneath the surface during the fallow season. Soil is being renewed, "the compilation of minerals, air, water, animals and other living matter that accumulates in layers and become compacted..". At the same time, the farmer is being renewed through a forced Sabbath. It is a time for both the land and the steward of the land to "wait upon the Lord".

Collison invites members of small rural churches to relive the seasons of fallow, planting, growing, and harvest in memory and imagination for the same of expanding the repertoire of their opportunities for action. The *God's Farm Study Guide* at the back of the book provides individual and group exercises to reinforce this journey of thought. How can a small rural church overcome its scripts of failure and find a hope that holds in season and out of season? The answer may be as close as the fields visible outside the clear glass sanctuary windows or the corn shock leaning against the altar in September. As near as the pungent smells of spring rain or autumn decomposition. As relevant as the drama of failed crops and lost family farms. Lean in close to the land, this book argues. Learn from the farmer's cycle of growth as though it were a template designed by God to prosper also the small local church.

Lew Parks

Professor of Church Leadership and Congregational Development, Emeritus Wesley Theological Seminary

ACKNOWLEDGMENTS

It takes many hands for a farm to yield something that brings life. And I am thankful for those who have helped in the process that brought this published work to fruition. First and foremost, I thank God from whom all blessings and good gifts flow by His grace and for His glory. Also, thank you to Trilogy Publishing for taking the step of faith in offering me the opportunity as a new author.

To Etta Todd, thank you for your gift of friendship, then and now, and your excellent proofreading skills, all which have kept me straight through all my writing drafts.

To Dr. Lewis Parks, Dr. Sathi Clarke, and my D.Min Story and Spirituality cohort at Wesley Seminary, thanks for the challenge to go deeper and wider in exploring my theology from new perspectives. To those small churches on the Dover District of the Peninsula Delaware Conference of the United

Methodist Church who willingly shared their time and their stories: Wesley UMC in Georgetown, Zoar UMC in Millsboro, Prospect UMC in Harrington, and Concord UMC in Seaford—thank you for helping me to help others.

I am grateful to my Dad whose stories planted a love of reading and writing in me at an early age as he and Mom nurtured my love of learning. Thank you to my in-laws, Eunice and the late Ronnie Collison, and all the Collisons who showed me how the rhythm of faith, family, and farm come together in every season of life. To my sons, Randy, Robby, Patrick, and Joe— it's been your willingness to transition from being a teacher's kid to a preacher's kid, and your grace through my "I have an idea" moments that gave me the encouragement to put pen to paper. And to Glenn, the man who has shown his support through the many days when papers and books had to be moved from the dining room table to make room for a late dinner, your love and encouragement made this work happen.

While I apologize for not including those who have

encouraged me, believed in me, prayed for me, or simply said, "you go, girl," know that I thank you for giving of yourselves to make the garden of ideas grow into this book.

Rebecca "Becky" Kelly Collison

INTRODUCTION

My love for stories began at a young age. Growing up in the small town of Laurel, Delaware, stories could be found everywhere I went. From the country market where I bought penny candy to the farmers gathered at the local Southern States shooting the breeze to testimony time at our country church, stories surrounded me. But my favorite stories were the ones told by my father.

My father worked shift work at the area factory, so he wasn't always able to put me to bed. On those occasions when he was home at that time, he often read poems and stories to me; but the best nights were when he told me stories of his own creation. At times during my childhood, my grade school classmates and even the members of my elementary Sunday school class shared in my delight as my father spun a tale that was laid on his heart. The characters in his stories were fictional and yet they were familiar. My father's stories usually began with a person facing a challenge and, through interactions with other characters and situations, met the challenge by showing the strength of goodness and kindness. As I grew older, those stories ended and were replaced with true stories about people he met and incidents he encountered.

After high school, my endeavors continued to include the power of story as I worked as a small-town newspaper reporter for five years and then embarked on my college journey, being the first member of my family to earn a bachelor's degree. Later, my career transition from special education teacher to United Methodist preacher saw my personal reclamation of the power of stories in life, but this time I was sharing the stories told in the Scriptures so others could connect the gospel of Jesus Christ to their everyday life. However, it took my entry into the doctor of ministry program at Wesley Theological Seminary to once again be reminded that story and spiritually healthy growth go hand-in-hand.

Having grown up within the agriculturally-rich community of lower Delaware, I realized time and time again that the farming landscape I took for granted was Jesus' most popular canvas for painting the gospel message of hope. My doctoral project involved some rural-based small churches in the local district of my annual conference, with a specific focus to my appointment to Wesley United Methodist Church, a small church within a rural town setting. I explain the steps I take for my project that I call, "Cultivating God's Farm: Using agricultural and biblical stories and seasons to reseed hope in small rural churches". The project took almost two years to fully complete from the initial idea and focus groups to final completion of studies in area churches. Qualitative and quantitative data is shared throughout the process and Bible study components. Additionally, the celebrations and failings of the project specific to Wesley UMC were shared.

Each generation has narratives that hold hopes, fears, history, and faith of people across the ages. Each person has a story, and each church has a story. And the best stories were the ones told when we were at a place where we were open to receive. The stories are heard in testimonies, in song, over a cup of coffee with a neighbor, and even in the midst of tears while sharing concerns in prayer time. Especially in the rural community where I grew up and have lived most of my life, relationships were made and strengthened by shared stories. The farmland found in abundance in the southern part of Delaware also told a story of seasons that are beyond human control but provide the necessary framework for the growth of fruit in the land. Our life narratives bear witness to who God is and who we are, for our stories are markers of where we have been and where we are going.

The doctoral project opened my heart and mind, not only to my own story but to my connection with others as they shared their stories. It is in community we see the image of God and it is through the stories of our experience, we can see the fullness of God. For the small rural church, it is a reminder we are a work that is still in process, a masterpiece still under creation upon the canvas of our current setting. As the land is a part of our lives in ways we may have forgotten or minimalized, helping the small and rural-based churches find their way amidst the seasons of change in the twenty-first century invites us to return to the land from where we have come to reclaim the life that is forever rooted in the echo of the garden of the Creator. So, come hear the story afresh and let it change your life.

CONTENTS

CHURCH, WE ARE GOD'S FARM

"A farm is a plot of land for growing things. The church is God's land to grow Christ, not in an individual way, but in a corporate way...something of Christ will be grown up in each of us".[1]

These words from Witness Lee speak to the understanding of God's Farm, the life found and offered in the relationship between Creator God and two interconnected creations: the land and humankind. Since the beginning, land has been a central theme in biblical faith and a key component in understanding humankind's relationship to God. Agrarian references throughout the Bible are not just a reflection of the economic and societal landscape from ancient times, but a template for one's individual spiritual growth in discipleship and for the growth of the church. Through the lens of the land, the human story of faith unfolds and informs the church today, specifically the small rural church that finds itself close to the land in agricultural regions.

The role of the land and its relevance to the lives of God's people can initially be seen throughout the Hebrew Bible. As author James Weldon Johnson referenced Genesis 2:7 in poetic verse:

> Up from the bed of river God scooped the clay;
>
> and by the bank of the river He kneeled him down;
>
> And there the great God Almighty
>
> ...kneeled down in the dust.
>
> Toiling over a lump of clay
>
> till he shaped it in his own image;
>
> then into it he blew the breath of life,
>
> And man became a living soul.[2]

Dietrich Bonhoeffer writes "humankind is derived from a piece of earth and its bond with the earth belongs to its essential being".[3] Bonhoeffer continues that "human beings have their existence as existence on earth".[4] From this agrarian viewpoint, the land-humankind connection goes deeper than

2

just God's creation of humankind's form out of dust. Ellen Davis, an agrarian theologian, explains the land-humankind connection in more detail.

> ...agrarians know the land, not as an inert object, but as a fellow creature that can justly expect something from us whose lives depend on it..". And YHWH God formed the human being ['adam], dust from the fertile soil ['adama] (Genesis 2:7) Although the wordplay is captured surprisingly well by the English pun "human from humus", the Hebrew is more fully descriptive of the family resemblance. Thus 'adam from 'adama is localized language; it evokes the specific relationship between a people and a particular place.[5]

From creation in the Garden of Eden to Noah's finding a place to land after the flood (Genesis 8), to Abraham's leaving his land of origin (Genesis 12), to Joshua setting foot upon the Promised Land (Joshua 1–5), humankind, namely God's people, have been connected to God through the land. The land—referenced as desert, orchard, fields, vineyards, mountains, and more—was seen as geographical and political property. The covenantal gift for Abraham, the inheritance of the Promised Land, meant stability and a place of physical belonging for God's people.

Theologian Walter Bruggeman notes that the "Hebrew term '*eres* functions to refer both to earth and land; in its usage as earth, the term clearly refers to the created earth with reference to the creator God who governs heaven and earth".[6]

He continues that the same term, however, refers to land, most specifically Israel's "land of promise" that Israel hopes for and holds from Yahweh. Bruggeman's assertion is that the land is for all heirs of the covenant, even those who have no power to claim it.[7] According to Bruggeman, the land for all is the single central symbol for the promise of the gospel.[8]

In the New Testament, the understanding of whom the land is for and what the land means to God's faithful takes on a new depth of significance. Jesus and his apostles developed a new understanding of the land, which saw the earlier particularistic focus on a physical land as a necessary means of preparing for God's purpose to "bless all nations" through Abraham's seed, the blessings of being "in the land" were now available universally through Israel's Messiah "in Christ".[9]

Jesus Christ brought the understanding of the life-giving land and its expanded role in spiritual growth and discipleship to his teachings in the New Testament. Jesus, who was born in a farm structure (Luke 2:7), taught with agrarian-based parables to help connect people of faith with the land to which they were inextricably connected by creation and by livelihood. These parables include:

- Grain on Sabbath, Matthew 12:1–8

- Sower, Matthew 13:1–9, 18–33

- Mustard Seed, Matthew 13:31–32

- Weeds in the Wheat, Matthew 13:24–39

- Worker in the vineyard, Matthew 20:1–16

- Tenants in the Vineyard, Matthew 21:33–46

- Budding Fig Tree, Matthew 24:32–35

- Rich Man and Bigger Barns, Luke 12:15–21

- Barren Fig Tree, Luke 13:6–9

- The Prodigal Son, Luke 15:11–24

Other agrarian references throughout the Gospels include the importance of the vine (John 15) and the role of the laborers for the Kingdom of God. (Matthew 9:27 and Luke 10:2)

For the people of the land to serve God, faith would

be required, and that faith would develop in cycles, much like the seasons of the agricultural landscape. Ecclesiastes 3 reminds us that "for everything, there is a season", and that as long as earth endures, the land will undergo seasons. (Genesis 8:22)

The land's agricultural seasons mirror the seasons of faith experienced by people of God throughout the Old and New Testaments. For the resident agrarian, the seasons are patterned in four basic stages: *fallow, planting, growing,* and *harvest* seasons. While each season may look different within different geographic areas, certain elements remain constant. Similar seasons are experienced in the spiritual lives of those created from the land; that is, all humankind and specifically God's people. By examining each season and its connection to the spiritual self, one can begin to see the correlation between the dynamics of the physical land and the spiritual life.

First, the *fallow season* is characterized by weather conditions and landscape that are not conducive to widespread planting in the outdoors, so empty fields are found. The time of not planting and not growing can be seen as a time of Sabbath for the ground. In Genesis, God rested on the seventh day. And in the Ten Commandments, God instructs us to do the same: "Remember the Sabbath day, to keep it holy. Six days you shall labor, and do all your work, but the seventh day is a Sabbath to the LORD your God" (Exodus 20:8). While even Psalm 23:2 suggests a Sabbath for the people, the land also must have a Sabbath, a time when planting and growing are not seen.

> But the seventh year you shall let it rest and lie fallow, so that the poor of your people may eat; and what they leave the wild animals may eat. You shall do the same with your vineyard, and with your olive orchard.

> Six days you shall do your work, but on the seventh day you shall rest, so that your ox and your donkey may have relief, and your home-born slave and the resident alien may be refreshed. Exodus 23:11–12 (NRSV)

Hymn writer Natalie Sleeth, who was in a season of feeling loss and grief following a friend's death,[10] remembered the line from a T.S. Elliot poem: "In my beginning is my end".[11] Sleeth wrote the "Hymn of Promise" which helps us understand the unseen power and hope of the fallow season:

In the bulb there is a flower; in the seed, an apple
tree;

In cocoons, a hidden promise: butterflies will soon
be free!

In the cold and snow of winter there's a spring that
waits to be,

Unrevealed until its season, something God alone
can see.[12]

The bare, empty field of uncertainty is also seen in scripture
passages such as Jeremiah 32 when God instructs Jeremiah to buy
land in a season that does not seem to be fruitful or promising to the
human eye. However, the fallow season of the land and the fallow
season of the spirit are necessary in the life of God's people.

Theologian Howard Thurman writes:

There is a fallow time for the spirit when the soil is
barren because of sheer exhaustion...whatever may be
the seasons, one has to deal with the fact. Face it! Then
resolutely dig our dead roots, clear the ground, but
don't forget to make a humus pit against the time when
some young or feeble plants will need stimulation from
past flowering in your garden....the time is not wasted.

The time of fallowness is a time of rest and restoration, of filling up and replenishing. It is the moment when the meaning of all things can be searched out, tracked down and made to yield the secret of living. Thank God for the fallow time.[13]

In agricultural and spiritual times, the fallow season is followed by a planting season. The planting season of the land is defined by favorable weather and landscape which show readiness to be turned over and plowed in order to receive seeds and new plantings. In the Old Testament, the prophet Hosea shows the connection between the planting season of the land and the planting season of the soul by referencing a time to "sow for yourselves righteousness; reap steadfast love; break up your fallow ground; for it is time to seek the LORD that he may come and rain righteousness upon you" (Hosea 10:12 NRSV).

Planting season is highlighted by the turning over of the ground to create new growth. In spiritual growth required in discipleship, to create or construct a new understanding, one must first destruct the current status quo from a new perspective, turn over the land for a fresh receptivity, and decide which seeds to plant based on the value of relationship

9

with God and others. Jesus as the Master Gardener cultivates the spiritual landscape in order to bring about new life. (John 12:23–24) The planting season is most clearly seen in scripture by the Parable of the Sower, which tells of seed that is broadcast and the state of the soil upon which it falls, in determining the fate of the seed in the physical and spiritual life of God's people. (Mark 4:3–9, 13–20; Matthew 13:1–9, 18–33) The planting season involves breaking up the hard ground to allow for gospel seeds to take root, removal of rocks that inhibit growth in challenging situations, and looking out for the thorns that choke out any fruit-bearing potential.

From the planting season, the land and the spiritual pilgrim must embark upon the *growing season*, a season characterized by the land which has received the seed and whereupon maturation from seed to plant takes place. Jesus' agrarian parables continue to address the growing season specifically with celebrations and challenges that accompany the physical growth on the land and the spiritual growth of the believer.

Celebration in the *growing season* is seen in the Parable of the Mustard Seed (Matthew 13:31–32), where the seed of little faith grows exponentially and benefits more than just the farmer. Challenges in the growing season are also apparent, as they are seen in the Parable of the Weeds in the Wheat (Matthew 13:24–39) and the Parable of the Barren Fig Tree (Luke 13:6–9) where the farmer in charge of monitoring the growth of the plant has to trust God's timing and God's plan, and not rely on one's own understanding of the growing process. These *growing season* parables inform individual believers and the church of what is required in order to bring about fruit for the kingdom.

The Apostle Paul also explains the dynamic between humans and God in the farming process:

> I planted, Apollos watered, but God [all the while] was causing the growth. So neither is the one who plants nor the one who waters anything, but [only] God who causes the growth. He who plants and he who waters are one [in importance and esteem, working toward the same purpose]; but each will receive his own reward according to his own labor. For we are God's fellow workers [His servants working together]; you are God's cultivated field [His garden, His vineyard], God's building. 1 Corinthians 3:6–9 (AMP)

In summation of the growing season, God does the growing but God's people have to be good stewards of the land given and the opportunities availed.

The fourth season of the land is identified as *Harvest;* a time when the growing period of a particular crop is completed and the crop taken out of the field to be dispersed in various ways. In the Old Testament, the harvest is described as a time of blessing for the one who planted (Deut. 24:19) and the one who didn't plant (Lev. 19:9). Specifically, the story of all of the seasons, and especially the significance of the harvest, can be seen in the Old Testament book of Ruth, a story that depicts the process from fallowness, to the planting of hope, to the growing of that hope, to the harvest of grain and of blessings to future generations. In the Ruth 2 passage, where Ruth is gleaning the fields, protection and provision are offered at the harvest as not only the lineage is protected, but generations to come will be provided by the fulfillment of the promised Messiah. But the harvest is not just about bringing in crops for the present age; the spiritual harvest is dependent upon the state of our heart, as seen in Jesus' parable about the Rich Man and the Bigger Barns. As God stands in control of the harvest (Jeremiah 5:24, Amos

4:7), so Jesus is the Lord of the harvest of God's kingdom (Matthew 9:38).

The Apostle Paul's writing in 1 Corinthians spells out the importance of the land in God's purpose for believers:

> Do not be deceived; God is not mocked, for you reap whatever you sow.[8] If you sow to your own flesh, you will reap corruption from the flesh; but if you sow to the Spirit, you will reap eternal life from the Spirit.[9] So let us not grow weary in doing what is right, for we will reap at harvest time, if we do not give up.[10] So then, whenever we have an opportunity, let us work for the good of all, and especially for those of the family of faith. Galatians 6:7–10 (NRSV)

As land is created by God, humankind is created of the land and given life by God, and is thereby connected to the land both physically and spiritually; in short, we are God's farm for a purpose—a reality that has been seen through the ages.

Through the years and across continents, the farming frontiers have been a canvas upon which the agrarian theologian made his point with broad strokes. One notable feature of nineteenth-century America was the ever-receding "American frontier" and the mentality it created. It provoked the growth of missionary endeavor and reinforced "varied, experience-based, and rather individualistic approach to spirituality".[14]

Through the formative years of the American landscape, the relevance of the agricultural landscape upon the faith is acutely understood by the people who claim small rural churches as their home and identity. The small rural church played a significant role in the circuit rider tradition in the early years of the Methodist movement. As the circuit rider would go from town to town in the early days of America's expansion, so the message of the Gospel would be seeded, planted, nurtured, and grown. One specific method of growth could be found in the camp meetings. Frederick Norwood writes: "Camp meetings were the few occasions when people were gathered, together in large numbers. Camp meeting time came "between the wheat harvest, and the time for gathering corn".[15]

Research from 2016 reveals over fifty-eight percent of American churches are considered small churches.[16] While small churches make up about an eighty percent majority

14

of the churches in the United Methodist denomination, small churches in rural agricultural settings have faced their own challenges as they sought to grow within the changing landscape and to hold on to their spiritual grounding as the literal ground beneath their feet has changed in the past century. Even though the theological significance of the land has not changed, how society views the relevance of faith in the twenty-first century has shed a new emerging need for spiritual renewal and grounding in society, and specifically in small rural churches.

Bruggeman addressed the dilemma of changing sociopolitical and economic dimensions, noting that biblical faith and the God of the Bible cannot be left disconnected from real public life in the world.[17] Bruggeman continues that "Loss of place and yearning for place are dominant images in contemporary culture".[18] He posits that a sense of space is a primary category of faith: specifically, place is space that has historical meanings where some things have happened that are now remembered and that provide continuity and identity across generations.[19]

For Bruggeman, humanness, as biblical faith promises it, will be found in belonging to and referring to that locus in which the peculiar historicity of a community has been

expressed and to which recourse is made for purposes of

orientation, assurance, and empowerment.[20] Bruggeman

continues: Human connectedness to the land is suggested

in biblical language by a play on words. *'Adam,* that (is,

humankind, has a partner and made, *'adamah* (land)...a sound

theology requires honoring covenantal relationships. The

operating land ethic in our society denies that relationship

at an enormous cost not only to land but to our common

humanity.[21]

Bruggeman surmises that while society yearns for a

home, it is living in such a way-disconnected from the life-

giving land-that it is becoming homeless in a sense.[22]

The disconnection from the spiritual grounding of the

land, once known through the small church, has been directly

affected by the farm crisis and rural focus decline in recent

years. Author Kathleen Norris addresses this issue based on

her experience with the rural communities in the Midwest. In

her book, *Dakota: A Spiritual Geography,* she notes:

...while not minimalizing the sufferings inflicted on the

Native Americans, the farm crisis of the 1980s leads her to

believe that farmers are the next Indians...losing one's land and facing massive national indifference...one (person) asked the question, 'How many of us are going to stand beside the farmer and see justice done for these people?'[23]

She continues by sharing glimpses of hope, as seen through a small rural church called Hope that depicts the resiliency of the land with the resiliency of grounded faith in the rural-based faith community. She notes that the song "Nearer My God to Thee", is a rural hymn that the city people don't fully understand, but those who live close to the land embrace fully. She writes:

I wonder if a church like Hope doesn't teach the world in the way a monastery does, not by loudly voicing its views but existing quietly in its own place...I wonder if what Columba Stewart, a contemporary Benedictine has said about such earthy metaphors, that "the significance of field, vineyard and garden metaphors in biblical post-biblical texts...lies beyond their relevance to the agricultural economy of ancient peoples".[24]

Hope's people have become one with their place, she continues, and this is not romanticism but truth.[25] She continues:

Hope's people are traditional people, country people, and they know that the spirits of a place cannot be transported or replaced. A pastor who was raised on a farm in Kansas said the thought that made Hope special was that the members were "all or nearly all, totally dependent on the land". He didn't seem to mind that church attendance got sparse at haying time and at calving...[26]

Norris continues that Hope's members take seriously their responsibility as members of the world's diverse and largely poor human race.[27] As an example, she cites that while Hope's membership declined by nearly half in recent years, the amount the church donates for missions has increased every year.[28]

As Bruggeman posits, our lives are set between expulsion and anticipation, of losing and expecting, of being uprooted and re-rooted, of being dislocated because of impertinence and being relocated in trust.[29] To maintain our grounding, we need to return to our identity as those who Creator God formed from the earth and infused with God's own spirit. Theologian Jürgen Moltmann explains this grounding as humans seeing themselves as the product of nature and theologically as *imago mundi*.[30] Moltmann explains: Human beings as "a creature in the fellowship of creation..". before we interpret this as being as *imago Dei*, we shall see him as *imago mundi*—a being that can only exist in community with all other created beings and which can only understand itself in that community.[31]

Diana Butler Bass, in her book, "*Grounded: Finding God in the World—A Spiritual Revolution*", expands on the idea of our identity being spiritually founded with the earthen ground:

God is the ground, the grounding, that which grounds us. We experience this when we understand that soil is holy, water gives life, the sky opens the imagination, our roots matter, home is a divine place, and our lives are linked with our neighbors' and with those around the globe. This world, not heaven, is the sacred stage of our times.[32]

It is upon the earthy sacred stage that humanity's relationship with the land and with God coalesces through the stories of one who knows both intimately...the farmer. Although farmers have always known that one's life and destiny are tied to the health of the soil, much wisdom has been lost as technology-driven, single-crop, large-scale farming replaced more intimate connections with the land.[33]

Butler Bass explains in reference to Mark 4:8 that Jesus' seed is God's love and the soil is us, so the moral of the story is that we are not "soil-y" enough.[34] She writes: God is a dirt farmer, not a vegetable gardener. Soil is not sin. Soil is sacred, holy, and good. When we care for it, we are doing God's work. Soil is life. And it is time for us to reclaim the dirt.[35] Davis expands on how humankind can reclaim the dirt through the biblical story. She supports the theory that "the things the biblical writers must themselves have intended as important conveyors of meaning, become intelligible when the Bible is read from an agrarian perspective".[36] Davis writes:

What the Bible can offer us are "vision and principle", not solutions from the past. An agrarian reading of the Bible is not an exercise in nostalgia, although it is a significant part of work of memory, of imagination anchored (not mired) in the past. Agrarian theoria looks forward to a potentially healing future; it is informed by modern science and also by traditional patterns of thought and value, even

practices that have ensured through centuries and millennia—
if only among a remnant—and may yet be adapted to meet
present and future exigencies...Hebrew scriptures are land
centered in their theological perspective.[37]

Davis continues that Jeremiah 4:26 reflects the
accuracy of "the collapse of American farming communities,
the most rapidly disintegrating sector of the national
economy...the tragedy of the heartland is the conversion
of the family-based farming economy to 'agribusiness'".[38]
She adds that Israelites survived as farmers by becoming
intimate with the land, by learning to meet its expectations
and its needs, and by passing on their knowledge, with each
generation serving as the human "seed stock" indispensable
for the well-being of the next.[39] The passing of this
information was accomplished through the spirituality
involved within the act of storytelling.

The search for spirituality "brings down to earth,
plants the feet firmly on the ground, and allows a vision of
self as it is, as we are imperfect and ambiguous".[40] In this
search for spirituality, the story emerges from true speaking
and true thinking to create a connection between the land
from which humans were formed and the Spirit which brings

the form to life.[41]

It is with the sacred story of the land, interwoven with the biblical story that emerges in the reality of the small rural church, creating the seeding of spirituality necessary for faith to be grown. The relationship between the land and its seasons and faith in God, with its spiritual seasons, provides a grounding which the small rural church is uniquely designed to offer. Theologian Howard Thurman understood the sacred connection whereby life comes from our innate grounding with the earth and our Creator. He wrote:

God is the source of the vitality, the life, of all living things. His energy is available to plants, to animals, and to our own bodies if the conditions are met. Life is a responsible activity. What is true for our bodies is also true for mind and spirit.[42]

Life happens because the biblical stories are combined with the stories of the land for a holy connection. Those who live on the land are in tune with the power of community not for just accomplishing the task at hand in and out of season, but also for continuing the sacred stories which grow and feed one's faith in the one who is love.

Author Wendell Berry notes that a farmer's connection begins in love and that community is necessary to make "good farming" outlast the life of any good farmer.[43] He adds that the people are joined to the land by work, yet in its cultural aspect, the community is an order of memories, preserved consciously in instructions, songs, and stories, and both consciously and unconsciously in ways.[44] Berry notes the connection in verse:

> The grower of trees, the gardener, the man born to farming,
>
> Whose hands reach into the ground and sprout,
>
> To him the soil is a divine drug. He enters into death
>
> Yearly, and comes back rejoicing. He has seen the light lie down
>
> In the dung heap, and rise again in the corn...[45]

Author Daniel Stulac writes about his experience at a little country church, located in a rural community historically devoted to animal husbandry, which decides to hang a portrait of Christ the Good Shepherd in the front foyer of the chapel. He wrote that this faithful congregation chose to characterize its faith through a portrait of Christ the farmer:

> Christ, whose arms are wrapped around a sheep. Christ who knows late nights in the barn and early mornings in the pasture. Christ, who knows the backbreaking work of hay season. Christ, who knows the gut-wrenching worry of a failed harvest...Christ of the compost pile. Christ of the filthy fingernails...The gospel of Jesus Christ is a gospel of emplacement. It is good news born in a barn. It is a gospel of the ground.[46]

He continues:

> We are, quite literally, born of dust. But that does not mean we are only dust. Filled with the breath of God, we have a special vocation, too—to serve the garden in which God placed us, and to keep it well. We are creatures designed by God to have our hands dirty; we are intended for cultivation.[47]

Cultivation is a process by which soil is broken and turned over to allow for new growth. The biblical and agrarian stories within the walls of the small rural churches found in agricultural landscapes can help us once again claim our identity as a people whose spiritual grounding comes from the dirt to which we return. For the God who formed humankind in Eden, on purpose, is still cultivating our spirits in the farmlands where rural churches call home and where the stories remind us that we are all part of God's farm.

As a creation of the land, we experience a grounding in the identity we share with the Creator of the land. Therefore, it is important to know the difference between soil and dirt—the difference is key for healthy physical and spiritual growth. I researched the question from a scientific viewpoint and found an article by writer Janet Raloff explaining that soil and dirt are not synonymous. In her interview with Pat Megonigal, soil exhibit curator and member of Soil Science Society of America, dirt is actually displaced soil.

> Soil is the compilation of minerals, air, water, animals and other living matter that accumulates in layers and become compacted over time. When particles of that soil erode or are dug up, they lose the 'history' of their place...essentially their associations with particles that might have been above, below, and to their sides.
>
> It sounds like he's saying soil is the diverse but inte-

grated community of living and inanimate things that make up the ground beneath our feet. And dirt? It's a group of runaways or kidnapped individuals that can't easily be associated with where they were born or grew up. In a sense, they're particles that have been rendered anonymous.[48]

With this definition, I realized any study of the land through a theological lens meant that one must distinguish a church with a "soil" culture and a church with a "dirt" culture specifically in the realm of small rural churches where not all were alike in their level of health and vitality. A "soil" culture church recognizes the diverse and integrated community that is layered in history and defined by place: the *soil* church is alive and offers to share that life. A "dirt" culture church does not have the integrated layers of community and history and has no place to call home; the *dirt* church exists but is not life-giving and is essentially suffering from spiritual homelessness. In other words, soil lives while dirt exists.

With the soil-dirt definition, a process of linking the local churches story, the biblical narrative and the agrarian discourse was necessary for re-discovering the layers of stories and the life they give to the church, and that a single story told to the small rural church by the current culture was like the dirt that left one spiritually homeless. What may seem like a *dirt* church just existing on the surface, may actually be a *soil* church when its stories are shared to offer life. But to know the land, one needs to be in touch with the land.

To accomplish this in the local church, I used a LAND approach to address the current situation of a church I pastored called Wesley to determine the next faithful steps of bearing fruit on God's farm in any season. The following chapters will address each letter in the acronym LAND and additional resources are provided at the back of this book.

So who are we as a church? What do we do next? Let's go to the land and find out.

L: LISTENING TO AND LEARNING FROM THE LAY OF THE LAND

"First this: God created the Heavens and Earth—all you see, all you don't see...God looked over everything he had made; it was so good, so very good!" (Genesis 1:1,31 MSG)

It is not uncommon to find a farmer walking the property, row by row, day by day. Not only does the farmer do this to find the section of fencing where the cows got out or to see the blight on the beans up close, but to look and listen to the land. The land has stories to tell, but the farmer has to walk it, come in physical contact with it, and be in relationship with it in all seasons in order to learn from it. Listening to the land is not just an activity for when life feels good or when a person wants something from the land. When a person listens, they can hear the stories the land tells and the stories it doesn't tell. The same is said of the small rural church: it longs to be known and longs to be heard. With each small rural church unique in its own way, each leader must identify the season and the spiritual lay of the land before moving forward to reclaiming the land.

The connection between faith and farming runs deep in American history, and specifically, in the past and the present of small churches in rural settings. According to the US Department of Agriculture, rural America is defined by the multidimensional qualities of the area including social and economic integration within an area. But three key components include open countryside, rural towns with fewer than 2,500 people, and urban areas with populations ranging from 2,500 to 49,999.[49]

Over the years, small rural churches, like those in southern Delaware, have met with challenges from societal demands and economic struggles. In 2003, Lyle Schaller released a book titled, *Small Congregation, Big Potential*. In this book, he related that the most comprehensive recent census regarding religious congregations in the United States was conducted by the Glenmary Research Center for the year 2000. Schaller defines a "small church" including those congregations averaging 125 or fewer at the principal weekend worship service.[50]

One reason to use 125 rather than 100 in this definition is the growing agreement that an average worship attendance of 125 or more is the contemporary minimum to be able to economically afford, to justify in terms of the workload, and to attract, challenge, and retain a full-time and fully credentialed resident pastor. For the United Methodist Church, the proportion of its churches averaging 125 or fewer in worship was at seventy-eight percent.[51] And of the large percentage of small churches in the denomination, most were found in rural communities of 8,000 people or less.

The twenty-first century has made its mark on the small rural church and its role in society. Small town, agricultural-based communities saw an exodus of people to areas that offered more opportunities in the social and technological culture of the times, and with the exodus, some small churches found fewer people in the pews. Megachurches with digital screens, online live streaming and podcasts gave churchgoers more options than the single service at the small rural church. In 2009, 207 rural churches closed their doors. In the past decade, the number of rural congregations has declined by more than 3,000 to slightly more than 20,000 today. In recent years, United Methodist leaders, presiding over an aging denomination losing US members and resources, are asking the church to place a priority on building "vital" congregations, and to hold bishops and pastors accountable for membership growth. Many in the rural church feel they are being left behind precisely at their moment of greatest need.[52] The same sentiment is echoed by many smaller acreage farmers across the country, including those in southern Delaware.

To date, forty-two percent of the land in Delaware is farmland, with most of it found within the boundaries of the two lower of the three counties in the small state.[53] Sussex and Kent counties are the two lower counties in Delaware and make up the Dover District in the Peninsula Delaware Conference of the United Methodist Church. Sussex and Kent counties are in the top two percent of 3,079 US counties in value of vegetables sold, as Delaware ranks number one nationally in the value of agricultural products sold per farm and value per acreage of land.

As farmland gave way to housing development in the twentieth century, some owners saw less risk in selling property rather than depending upon the climate of the economic market and the uncertainties of the weather. Some farmers felt that rather than year after year putting in the hard work and long hours for the crop which may or may not make a livable profit, they would sell the land and be done with the uncertain seasons that inevitably emerged. However, the farmers determined to save the farmland came up with other solutions using current resources in new ways.

With a drop in the number of farms and acreage over the past one hundred years, Delaware became number one in the US based on the percentage of land in farms preserved.[54] The increase in farmland and the establishment of legacy farms are efforts to create vital farmland development and to stop the exodus of young farmers. Farmland preservation ensures the land will be used only for farming over the next century. The legacy farms promote generational farming. Likewise, new attention is being given to farm-to-table produce, emphasizing once again the importance of the fruit of the land for the people of the land, using the resources available in new ways and with a new focus.

L.H. Bailey once wrote "as a trustee of the land, a farmer must handle all his resources for a man cannot be a good farmer unless he is a religious man".[55] Just as farming is not just about the physical and monetary elements of bringing forth a crop, so the church must also realize it is not just about being a good steward of the property and monetary resources. Bailey continued: Into this secular and more or less technical education we are now to introduce the element of moral obligation that the man may understand his peculiar contribution and responsibility to society; but this result cannot be attained until the farmer and every one of us recognize the holiness of the earth.[56]

To address the issues related to the uncertainty of the seasons of rural agriculture, one must know the lay of the land and be familiar with its past as well as its present condition. Similarly, the rural church is in an uncertain season of existence yet has resources within its past seasons and the current "lay of the land" of its faith.

In the rural churches, the agricultural seasons of *fallow time, planting, growing,* and *harvest* find their resonance in the church calendar. Homecoming services are usually held at harvest time, when the corn, hay, and soybean crops are ready to be brought in. Fallow or wintertime, when the fields are bare, is when most of the farming community takes time off and church Bible studies are usually better attended. Planting season in the spring usually sees local farmers working longer days, often strategically planning to avoid spring rains. The growing season is a time of monitoring the plants but also offers time for gathering at the state fair or other events before the harvest season comes again.

Closeness to the physical land can draw one closer to the biblical significance found in agrarian scriptural references. Favorite songs include "In the Garden", "Trust and Obey", and "Great is Thy Faithfulness" while favored scriptures in the rural church tend to come from Genesis, Ruth, and from Jesus' agrarian parables. However, society demands that "bigger is better" and that "technology reigns" are such sentiments that have separated some rural churches from their grounding and inherent rootedness to the land. Masanobu Fukuoka, a farmer theologian, noted that "To the extent that people separate themselves from nature, they spin out further and further from the center".[57] He added that "farming used to be sacred work...Farming, as an occupation, this is within nature, lies close to this source".[58] To be connected with one's source is to be connected with one's identity.

In Lewis Parks' book, *Preaching in the Small Membership Church*, he posits that a small membership church pastor must take on the role of an anthropologist. He notes the pastor must uncover, name, and respect the identity of the church he or she serves.[59] Knowing the identity, or lay of the land in a church, can uncover untapped resources and begin the work and dealing with the challenges.[60] Goleman suggests "good storytelling can honor what they accomplished in the past, cull the wisdom that was there, and help reframe new practices for the future".[61] Mann notes that specific geographic setting is key to a congregation's story, since congregations are born from a generative spark of interaction between stories of faith and stories of place.[62] Mann continues that place-based narratives provide "here" with a trajectory that stretches over time including remembered past, present reality, and an outline of imagined futures.[63]

Mary Clark Moshella extends this idea of place-based narrative that is offered back to the congregation "speaking the truth in love (Ephesians 4:15) and with humility, expecting and facilitating further critique and dialogue".[64] She continues both pastor and people start to tap in to "the resources of theological imagination", new ideas and energy for change to emerge.[65]

In Berlin and Weems' book *High Yield*, leaders are reminded that ignoring the culture can be the downfall of wonderful visions for a newly imagined future. The authors relate the story of how a relatively new pastor was shown that culture matters to growth, as the new pastor proposed a specific community outreach program.

The response was always the same, "We're just farmers. We can't do what other churches do". This culture was new to the pastor...he started viewing the vision of outreach through the lens of their culture. Soon he realized that providing food for a range of people without sufficient food was a need in the community. A vision emerged around "food for the hungry". Sure enough, those who seemed instinctively to resist new ideas spoke up: "Pastor, we can't do that. We're just farmers". Immediately, the irony was evident to them and others. "Of course, we can do that. That's who we are. That's what we do. We are farmers. We feed the world.[66]

Berlin and Weems suggest that linking the rural

churches narrative to the gospel commandment "to go" and using the agricultural culture which defines them, can help align not only vision and culture but create a new narrative.[67]

Parks notes the small church is "the natural setting for soul care, the more favorable climate to engage persons whose life stories have been disrupted and now seek God's presence and leads as they dwell among a community of persons who share a common worship, Bible, sacraments, religious calendar, building, and assorted projects of discipleship".[68] He continues that the small church maintains its spiritual life and practices "in season and out of season".[69]

To learn the lay of the land, one must look and listen before making plans. The first thing to look to is to know what season the church is currently in and the state of its groundedness. For example: is it a dirt church without life-giving layers or a soil church that has multiple rich layers?

Looking around to see how the congregation reflects its community is the first step. Walking the land and seeing what is and is not there can be done by individuals or by groups of people in the church. It is helpful to employ the eyes of veteran saints and of newcomers for each offer a different perspective to be offered for a more complete picture. However, I found the stories to be the most telling of the current lay of the land. To focus these stories from a spiritual perspective, I employed a method called story linking used by Anne Streaty Wimberly in her book, *Soul Stories*.

The strength of the story-linking process is seen when the agricultural narrative is connected to the faith stories of small and rural-based churches. Stories shared from beauty salons to bean fields may vary in focus from the climate affecting the field to the climate affecting the legislative assemblies, but all help form the identity of a people. While some stories are painful and others buried under a protective veneer, the leadership of the church had been struggling with ways to bring forth their story and hear God's voice anew. The story-linking process with the culturally specific agrarian-based narrative allowed the reclamation of what is sacred, organic, and real; in essence, the process promoted their connection to each other, to God, and to the land in an increasingly technological world that seems to have forgotten its roots.

Author Anthony Pappas contends that each church,

with its mix of the common and the individual, has its own

story, its own script, and its own future.[70] Small churches

have not only a unique story but unique resources even in

current times. Small churches have a unique ministry in the

twenty-first century. Much of what they have to offer is what

they have always had to offer, the incarnation of the living

presence of God in real social relationships...the primary

quality of small churches is their relational dimension.[71]

Saint Paul had said that we—God's people, the

church—are God's farm (1 Corinthians 3:9 NCV), so the

same principals of reclaiming farmland in God's name

could help reclaim the spiritual vibrancy that identifies

even the small rural church as God's people called to bear

fruit. Author Noah Sanders notes four basic principles of

biblical world view of agriculture: We don't own our farm

(Genesis 1:26); farming is not about us (Luke 12:15–21);

God knows more about farming than we do (Romans 1:20);

and we can't make things grow (1 Corinthians 3:7).[72] The

same agricultural principals apply to the small rural church

in today's culture: if we want our churches—even small

rural churches—to produce the fruit that God desires, then

they need to acknowledge the basic principles related to the church as God's Farm (1 Corinthians 3:9 NCV) and be rooted in the soil of the Word of God. Sanders continues that one needs to "keep tabs on the condition of the different parts of our farm" and not assume that everything is just going fine and it will keep going fine (Proverbs 27:23–24).[73] Likewise, small rural churches cannot assume everything is going fine but instead must know the lay of the land where God has placed them and acknowledge its current state.

Masanobu Fukuoka, in *The One Straw Revolution,* wrote "the ultimate goal of farming is not the growing of crops but the cultivation and perfection of human beings".[74] The connection of soil and spirit is expanded by Wendell Berry:

> The soil is the great connector of lives, the source and destination of all. It is the healer and restorer and res-urrector, by which disease passes into health, age into youth, death into life. Without proper care for it we have no community because without proper care for it we have no life.[75]

To know the lay of the land, one must physically be in contact with the land and experience its past and its present to acknowledge where one truly is in their journey. Only then can the spiritual farmer move forward in planning and plowing for new fruit to be brought forth.

A: ASSESSING AND ACKNOWLEDGEMENT OF THE GROUND AND ITS IDENTITY

"He taught them many things by parables, and in his teaching said: "Listen! A farmer went out to sow his seed.."". (Mark 4:2–3 NIV)

Any farmer knows not everything grows well everywhere. Rice likes to grow in a wet environment, but wheat needs a dryer landscape. Over the years, I have seen pastors upon getting to a new church appointment, begin putting plans and programs into place because their plan or another pastor's plan worked on a different plot of God's farm. Churches in general can't adapt to a one-size-fits-all approach and this is very true for the small rural church. After taking the time to know and learn the lay of the land and in what season the church found itself, I began to address that season and call it what it was. For example, if the pews are sparsely populated and there is no study or outreach underway, most likely the church is in a fallow season. Likewise, if ideas are springing up, new people are coming in, and still some people are complaining that "We've never done it that way", the church may be in the early stages of a growing season.

Addressing the appropriate season then lends to acknowledging that season. By definition, the verb "to acknowledge" means to accept or admit the existence or truth of a situation. One example of acknowledgment may be noting a dirt landscape as having rocky areas where one may need to spend extra time removing obstacles; it does no good to start planting spiritual seeds if the land is not ready to let those roots go deep. Likewise, one should acknowledge the dry areas that need more "living water" saturation by means of healing and assurance, the poor soil areas that need rich nutrients found in a vibrant spiritual relationship with Christ, and the hard soil that needs to be humbly and gently broken so it can be turned over and make room for new life to occur.

As was mentioned in the growing season, there are challenges that emerge to stop the change from seed, to rooted plant, to full-fledged crop; one cannot stop because of the challenges but take them in stride as the wheat and weeds are grown up together with grace. One needs to recognize the celebrations and the challenges of being faithful in the season you are in instead of wanting to be somewhere else. Once a leader is in relationship with and learning from the land, and addresses the current situation accordingly, then comes the third step.

To help Wesley United Methodist Church find its future, amidst the landscape of rural farmland and faith in twenty-first century southern Delaware, I began to listen to the story of where the church had come from and where it was currently grounded. While I heard stories about the glory days from fifty years earlier, I also heard the absence of stories about how the Spirit had moved in more current times. Annual reports showed a steady decline in attendance over the previous twenty years, gradual but declining nonetheless. The fiscal budget for the past decade had been based on "what we needed" instead of a realistic projection of antic-ipated giving; therefore, the budgets were often in the red. During the decade of budget decline, additional conference support was required. In some of those years, apportionments to conference were only partially paid.

Difficulties began to surface in the day-to-day operations of the church. The boiler was only operating at forty percent efficiency creating large, ominous heating bills during the winter months. Cosmetic fixes within the structure that had been left for a time when more funds were available were now becoming necessary repairs. As the church building seemed to become less efficient from a heating and maintenance perspective, the spiritual life of the congregation had begun to fade. The congregation's identity was rooted in past pastors, past church leaders who had gone on to glory, and past achievements. However, inside the building, empty pews and blank spaces on the leadership and committee rosters told a different story for current times. Overall, the church was full of good people with good intentions but the fear that accompanied monetary concerns and the church's aging facility needs became a primary focus. Spiritual formation necessary to grow as disciples and to subsequently make disciples was a distant second.

Throughout my life, when I needed to clear my head, walking those fields—whether freshly plowed, expectant with seed embedded beyond my sight, or knee high with soybean plants—there was a peace, a connectedness with

God that I would take for granted and not reclaim until I was much older and wiser. As a United Methodist pastor now back in the agricultural landscape that helped create me, I found a small rural church that I loved struggling with the season in which it found itself.

Howard Thurman tells the story about a pecan tree that relates to this situation:

> I watched him for a long time. He was so busily en-gaged in his task that he did not notice my approach until he heard my voice...He was an old man—as I discovered before our conversation was over, a full eighty-one years. Further talk between us revealed that he was planting a small grove of pecan trees. The little treelets were not more than two-and-a-half or three feet in height. My curiosity was unbounded.

> "Why did you not select larger trees so as to increase the possibility of your living to see them bear at least one cut of nuts?

> Finally, he said, "These small trees are cheaper, and I have very little money".

> "So, you do not expect to live to see the tree reach

sufficient maturity to bear fruit?

"No, but is that important? All my life I have eaten fruit from trees that I did not plant; why should I not plant trees to bear fruit for those who may enjoy them long after I am gone? Besides the man who plants because he will reap the harvest has no faith in life.[76]

Thurman concludes that all of life is a planting and a harvesting. No man gathers merely the crop that he himself has planted; this is another dimension of the brotherhood of man.[77] Thurman's story is a reminder that growth and health can never be dependent upon one person or one planting.

While the saints and previous church leaders of Wesley United Methodist Church had been faithful in planting in earlier years, the following generations reaped the harvest but forgot to replant with the intention that the yield is not specifically for them in their time. The church's past approach was seen in limited risk-taking, internal focus, and fundraisers for the church to meet its bills. Few mission-related endeavors were attempted in those years, and of the ones that were, risk was minimal. Financial focus obscured some of the necessary faith-development focus needed to sustain and grow a healthy and spiritually vibrant church.

In short, opportunities were missed to see what God wanted to do because the focus was on the church trying to do all the work with the church's minimal resources of finances and people. And even so, God seeks to reveal Himself to His people through the small rural churches that are so abundant in the Methodist denomination, across the country, and even across my local district. Hope and faith are priorities for the farmer tending the land; hope and faith should also be priorities for the small churches located on the land.

With the source of the culture and economy being rooted in the surrounding land, the source of the spirituality of God's people could also be rooted in that same land but from a slightly different perspective. Place-based narratives are resources to consider that emerge in the rich stories from one's own backyard, a backyard created specifically by God for "such a time as this". Narratives help identify what has been and can help create a future narrative built on hope and faith.

If the Bible and the land reflect the seasons of our lives, would the combination of stories and seasons also give direction for cultivating spirituality to bring hope and health into the church's current situation? To answer this question, I needed to look closer at the land and how to work this plot of God's farm called Wesley. I also had to take on a farmer's mentality and process.

Growing up in southern Delaware, I observed that farmers have different roles in different seasons. In the winter when the fields are fallow, farmers took the time to get equipment ready for the upcoming season; this was also the time for farmers to rest and reflect while letting nature take the rested land and breathe new life into it. The fields looked empty and bare, and yet the farmer knew that there was transformation occurring under the surface.

In the spring, the equipment was used to prepare the ground by cultivating it or turning it over to plant seeds. Seed was chosen for a specific need and tailored to the environment where it could thrive. Fertilizer and other nutrients were applied to help the seed die to self and grow into the plant it was destined to become.

Summer saw the growth of crops, often accompanied by the presence of new challenges. During the growing season, farmers protected their crops from damage by weeding and treating for insects. Invariably, some crops were lost but many continued to grow due to the constant attention on bringing the crop to its full potential. While the farmer didn't make the plants grow, it was the farmer's responsibility to be diligent and proactive.

When fall came with its cooler temperatures, harvest was the focus of the farmer. The entire farming community seemed to be fully involved in the hard work of getting the crop from field to table in a timely manner. Timing was essential because of the uncertainty of the weather that could destroy the yield. While the seed died to itself when planted in the ground months before, the fully-realized plant was called to die to itself once again at the harvest. However, each time it died, a new opportunity for future growth was generated.

After talking to the people in rural areas, especially those involved in some level of farming or gardening, I realized the rural-based church experienced the same changes in their spiritual life as a plot on God's larger farm. I then wondered if using the farmers' response to the seasons as a model would help cultivate the fields of the small country churches. To test the theory and try the farming model on the church's spiritual seasons, I would first need to define the seasons that are specific to the church. So, my first step was to determine where Wesley was in its spiritual life.

I turned my attention to create more of a relational, small group approach with a different type of study format to infuse the discipleship process with a spiritual practice via stories. Bible studies in the church had typically been a lecture format with a question and answer response. A different type of study would need to include guided discussion and the encouragement to tell stories from the participants' own experience. The format would highlight stories from the seasons of the lives of individuals, of the church, of the community, and link them with scriptural text and present location.

Much like a farmer who literally does not put all of his eggs in one basket, I could not seek healthy growth in only one area of the church. Farmers I knew had a main crop like feed corn, but also had one section of the farm for a smaller, secondary crop like watermelons and an area for the hogs or cows. The diversification used in farming is used as a safeguard if disease or low prices put the farm in financial difficulty; it also allows for the farm to offer more than just one product. Building upon this idea, I began looking at a variety of ways across the life of the church to best prepare the land known as Wesley UMC to move from a *fallow* season to a *planting* season.

Before starting to plant any seeds, I knew that Wesley needed to rest from its years of trying to rely upon its own power to make growth happen. The equipment used by Wesley (the church building) needed some attention for the anticipation of a future planting season, so the to-do list quickly grew into a Capital Improvement campaign. Meanwhile, taking the Scripture verse, "Be still and know that I am God" (Psalm 46:10) to heart, the practice of prayer was re-introduced as a manner of hearing from the land and its Creator God.

With the absence of any kind of organized prayer focus in the church, I began treating each layer of the church with prayer in all areas of church life. With no ongoing prayer team in place, prayer became a priority to ready the land for future growth. At this point, the lay of the land showed where worship attendance had been in steady decline for over a decade and where the past decade of church expenses exceeded the realized income and left the church often operating in a deficit. As in many cases, when money becomes a primary concern in the church, discipleship and spiritual growth can often take a distant second.

The spiritual discipline of prayer was heavily emphasized in worship, in studies, and even in the business meetings of the church. By saturating the ground with the rich spiritual nutrients of prayer and by getting the church ready to receive, we knew we were getting ready to plant. As each specific seed is planted for a purpose, I had to be intentional about the seed or actions that would yield the spiritual growth the church needed. Expensive projects, programs, or consultants were not in our budget, but we had a bag of seed that had been handed down and was ready to deploy.

To accomplish meaningful cultivation of the church's spiritual landscape, I would employ the power of stories in a different kind of small group study. The study group offered direction for the planted seeds of the personal, biblical, and agricultural stories to create a hybrid of new growth; new growth that could give new hope and health to the church. The small group format combined accountability and support to watch over and nurture one another in the process.

For the task to be measurable and able to be used by other small churches for understanding their own identity in relationship to the physical land and being God's field, I would create a Bible study that included stories. The study would yield qualitative and quantitative data for the pastor and the local pastor of the small rural church to use as a tool to turn over the soil in their own tract of God's farm. Since stories come at no financial cost, any small church could use the guided discussions and stories to help understand where they had been, where they are, and how to proceed faithfully in the current season. Every season has its celebrations and challenges; therefore, any season a church finds itself in has potential for growth if one follows the markers.

Many people familiar with the look of a plowed field were actually amazed at how straight the lines of planted seed are arranged. The straight lines of most fields were made possible by ridge markers that mark where the center of the tractor should drive (while planting) on the next pass after the one the farmer is currently on. In this manner, each row would be lined up perfectly parallel to the one just before it. The farmer went through a methodical process of taking each row at a time, one by one and side by side. Taking the cue from the farmer's planting process, the small church realigns itself to its mission, one row at a time. Since prayer is the standard set in Scripture over and over again, it became the marker with which the church set to ready the field for the seed the varied stories would bring.

With the abundance of stories emerging from personal experience, scripture, and the rural landscape around the church, I employed an adapted story linking method that could help create a new narrative for the church.

The story linking process was originated by Anne E. Streaty Wimberly within her study found in "Soul Stories: African American Christian Education". She explains:

> Story-linking is a process, whereby we connect parts of our everyday stories with the Christian faith story in the Bible and the lives of exemplars of the Christian faith outside the Bible. In this process, we link the Bible stories by using them as mirrors through which we reflect...by linking with Christian faith heritage stories,

we may be encouraged and inspirited by predecessors who have faced the circumstances with which we readily identify. The story-linking process can help us open ourselves to God's call...[78]

Wimberly's focus was to "bring forth liberating wisdom and hope-building vocation" by linking stories in the life of the people. Specifically, she connected the everyday story, the biblical story, and then added the culturally-specific story of the African-American faith heritage to reveal a way to authentically live in the image of Jesus Christ.

My adaptation of Wimberly's process also uses the linking of the everyday story with the Biblical narrative but then, after linking those two stories, view them through an agrarian-based narrative with the final link being made with a concrete action bridging the congregation and community.

By replacing Wimberly's focus on the culturally-specific story of the African-American faith heritage with the culturally-specific focus of the agricultural narrative, the stories would more readily resonate with those in small rural or country churches. Stories rooted in the land where the people lived, worked, and worshipped permeate the community and would create a cohesive thread to connect with the land and its Creator God.

To begin this type of approach, an overview of the story-linking process was necessary. Wimberly's approach focused on four components in the story-linking process, with the first being engagement of the everyday story. She began with the understanding that every person has a story that defines who they are and how they got here, a narrative that has been influenced by other narratives gleaned from social contexts, life events, and interpersonal relationship—all the pieces that form one's identity. When expanding that idea in working with congregations, one must understand "story is the way a community usually views, values, and talks about itself in relation to its world and heritage".[79] To name the everyday story requires one to identify with one of the other narratives to reveal the unfolding story plot. For example, in working with my congregation, I used their identity in light of how they see themselves within their interpersonal relationship to their community. The everyday story in the linking process to be used in the small rural churches is the story that the local church tells about a particular season in its particular history. To name the everyday story in a study format, it was helpful to have a preconstructed everyday story offered by the leader which reflected the narratives told in relation to the season being addressed.

The study was conducted over a nine-month period in four different churches.[80] Each church met for six nights for approximately sixty to seventy-five minutes. Each night, the session began with the opening page that included a visual representation to help initiate dialogue. A teacher's guide also gave background and a prayer exercise that can be used for each session at the facilitator's discretion. Directions, with related stories and scriptures, are written on the pages so the study could be self-led but does yield better results when a small group is able to discuss and share together.

The dynamic of the small group provides fertile ground for stories to be told. As Sensing writes:

> We all have stories existing and being created in each socio-historical context, accordingly our future stories are continuously written and constructed through dialogical human interaction and a dialogue of multiple voices. Narratives foster listening to the multiple voices emanating from ever emerging and developing

contexts. When people let you hear their stories, they are sharing a sacred trust, for it is through their stories they give meaning and interpret their lives.[81]

The first session is an introduction to the importance of land to our identity as a people and church, and how our relationship with the land connects with our relationship with God. In the first session, the idea of seasons of the land and seasons of spirituality within our personal and corporate church lives is introduced. For the days directly following the session, a section called "Gleanings" was included for optional contemplation and prayer focus. In the first session, all participants were encouraged to share their understanding of the word "heir" and how that related to their lives and their churches. Specifically, they shared what they hoped to hand down to the next generation. The groups also explored what the land meant to them and many shared that when they needed to get centered or connect with God, they returned to the land via the mountains, the lake, the beach, or simply the field behind their home. Specific comments related to the land included:

- It reminds me of things that matter.
- I feel closer to God.

- There is something renewing and therapeutic about putting your hands into the dirt.

- I love going to the chicken house and dealing with the chickens; no one seems to follow me there.

- God's calling to me came when I was on the lake.

- There is something sacred about just climbing a tree: the touch, the height, the view.

- I go for a walk when dealing with stress or to clear my head.

Then the participants were asked to share why their church was in the physical location it was; in other words, what role did the land play in the church being planted in its current location.

Wesley, with current average worship attendance of ninety-two, claims this location was the third in its lifetime and it was where the people were as Georgetown grew from a village into a town.

For Zoar, with an average worship attendance of fifty, the location was donated in the late 1700s or early 1800s, and the church was built with contributions of material and labor on the location that was an early camp meeting area. The original structure burned down but the members rebuilt the structure that remains today.

Concord, with an average worship attendance of fifty, a small unincorporated community in western Sussex County, originally had several bog-iron furnaces in the area in the late eighteenth century due to its close proximity to the river. However, when the railroad came to nearby Seaford, commerce and growth moved away. The small church stands today in the midst of a dozen homes.

For Prospect, with its average worship attendance of sixty-five, the church was located on donated farmland at the time of the Civil War (1850s) and remains surrounded by cornfields today. With the exception of additional attached rooms and updated plumbing and electric, the building remains true to its origins.

As the first session concluded, one pastor pulled me aside to tell me that she was pleased with the interaction at the initial session. She said that usually she had a difficult time getting participants to join in discussion and dialogue during a Bible study, but everyone at this study was engaged and felt they had something to offer. She left pleased and I left hopeful.

The second session focused on the first of the four seasons to be addressed: the *fallow* season. From an agrarian perspective, the fallow season is when fields are bare and nothing seems to be growing. For many in the mid-Atlantic region, this season is known as winter. Using the image of a fallow field, participants were asked to give physical, emotional, and spiritual descriptors of the season. All groups shared descriptors such as sad, cold, bare, anxious, wanting, dormant, time of rest, and a time of reflection. Some participants noted this was their least favorite season; but others found it as a much-needed season due to the ability to rest from certain jobs or projects on the farm.

When asked what the *fallow* season looks like in the local church, responses included a sense of grieving and hard truths, cold empty pews, not seeing activity, time of division, discouraging, unwelcoming, fear of unknown, lack of growth, and lack of communication. At this point, the everyday story from the *fallow* season was shared and groups were encouraged to match up the descriptors they named with the elements they heard in the story. This activity then prepared them to recount a *fallow* season they experienced in their own church. Loss of certain ministries, the change of pastors, and decline in attendance and finances were noted among the individual church's story of its *fallow* season.

From this point we moved into the story found in Jeremiah 12:1–25 and Exodus 23:11–12. In smaller breakout groups or pairs, the participants read the scripture and discussed what was going on in the story, who was in the story, and how the descriptors for the fallow season could be seen in the story. Within this dialogue, links between the descriptors, the everyday story, and the biblical story were being made. As the group gathered back together to share, the question was asked, "Where is God in the *fallow* season as seen in the everyday story and the biblical narratives?" Many responded that the fallow season may not seem to have a positive aspect, but it is in the fallow season that the ground is renewed to ready itself for the next planting. It was also noted that the fallow season provided downtime and Sabbath to wait on God and strengthen trust in God. One person wrote:

> Snow is a distinctive feature of the winter season.
> While the ground is fallow, the snow is nature's own
> fertilizer. As the snow melts, it not only waters the

ground but any farmer knows it infuses nitrogen into the ground naturally, thus making the soil richer for when the planting season comes around. It may not be our way or our time, but God's way and God's time is always best.

At this point, the culturally specific story in the story linking process was shared and further linking was made in relation to the fallow season. One woman from Prospect shared that the fallow season gives us a chancee to restore and regenerate because the consequence is that we can burn out and not be productive if we don't slow down so we have to step back to let God be God.

As a conclusion to the session on the fallow season, the participants were asked "what message emerges for you from the fallow season" and "how do we live faithfully in the fallow season"? Responses varied for each church situation, but the overall theme was for God's people to be patient, for we may grow but we need to have hope for loss can lead to restoration, reformation, or recreation. Other responses included the reference to songs like "Hymn of Promise" and "Blessings" by Laura Story.

The third session of the study addressed the *planting*

season. The image of artist Vincent van Gogh's 1888 painting

called *The Sower* was presented on the opening page for

the planting season and was used as part of a *visio divina*

(divine seeing) reflection and prayer. From an agricultural

perspective, the *planting* season is when ground is turned

over to make room for a new planting and plans are put

into motion to fertilize and nurture the new growth. In the

planting season, a farmer must often cultivate—pull up and

turn over—the soil by reshaping it so it can accept the seed

and water needed to grow. For many in the Mid-Atlantic

region, this season is experienced as spring. Using the image

of a *planting* season field, participants were asked to give

physical, emotional, and spiritual descriptors of the season.

All groups shared descriptors such as being busy, seeing

plowed rows and hearing tractors, anticipation of warmer

weather, weather beginning to change, being intentional,

fresh earthy smell, rejuvenation, new life, desire to get out

and go. One person in the Prospect study noted that when

the dirt was turned over, it looked different because it went

from dry brown to moist black with the promise of growth to

come. Another participant from Zoar noted that it's amazing

how everything grows once the soil is turned over, but it also sometimes gets stinky in the process.

When asked what the *planting* season looks like in the local church, responses included the emergence of new ideas for outreach and ministry, renovation projects, and deciding which seeds to plant intentionally and faithfully. Prospect participants noted a time when they walked around town handing out invitations to Vacation Bible School, and while that one action didn't yield any new attendees, they said they were reminded we do not always see the result of seeds planted. One noted that like the walnut tree that takes fifty years to grow to the point it bears fruit, the seeds we plant are always dependent on the climate and the timing. Concord noted that in turning ground over to provide for new growth in the church, things can get stinky, but you just have to step forward and break ground, letting God specialize in deepening and strengthening the roots.

As the third session focused on the *planting* season progressed, the story-linking process brought in the biblical text from Jesus' parable of the sower in Mark 4:3–9, 13–20 and John 12:24. Once again, smaller breakout groups or pairs were created where the participants read the scripture and discussed what was going on in the story, who was in

the story and how the descriptors for the *fallow* season could

be seen in the story. Within this dialogue, links between the

descriptors, the everyday story, and the biblical story were

being made. As the group gathered together to share, the

question was asked, "Where is God in the planting season as

seen in the everyday story and the biblical narratives?"

From the parable, a discussion of the soils was

applied to the challenges in the planting season in the

agricultural setting and in the local church setting. All agreed

that the John scripture was a reminder that just as a seed

needs to die to be born into a new life, we too need to die

to ourselves spiritually and the process of planting requires

either time, energy, or effort be given up from all of us. One

Wesley participant noted that "life has ups and downs and my

life is a field constantly getting turned over, so I have to trust

God, have faith, and seek him before I make my plans". The

participant went on to share that sorghum—a type of grain

similar to corn—grows in quantity but is not as profitable

because the nature of the crop "gums up" everything so it

takes a lot more to make it profitable; in like fashion, we

need to be prayerful of what we plant and why because the

need may be present but may require more of us than we are willing to give.

In sharing the agricultural-based narrative, which shares challenges of the *planting* season, the theme that resonated was that we must be intentional, flexible and patient as we do what we can and leave it with God. The song, "Great is Thy Faithfulness" and "Trust and Obey" are songs that resonated with whether we are doing new things, or other things in a new way, we must pray for God's guidance first and continue to plant seeds to God's glory. One participant shared the following reflection:

> When my boys were little, there was a corn plant that grew next to the mailbox. We didn't know how it got there. But there it stood all by itself. The mailman commented on it. The neighbors commented on it. One day, my little boy, Scotty, said, "It's mine, Momma". "I put it there. I planted it near the mailbox". So, we made a sign that said, "Scotty's Corn" and, don't you know, that one stalk actually even grew ears of corn. Goes to show if you plant a seed, it doesn't matter where, growth can happen.

The message that emerged from all the groups was that in the *planting* season, we need to be intentional and go forth and plant, and not just hope something grows. Each church group then went on to explain their reasons why that might or might not happen. Many in each group noted that the seasonal bugs of "we've never done it that way before" always seemed to emerge in this stage. One church noted the age of its membership, while another church noted its close proximity to a heavily Spanish-speaking neighborhood could create communication problems.

The fourth session of the study addressed the *growing* season. The image of a farmer overlooking a field of growing crops was used to help initiate conversation. From an agricultural perspective, the growing season is defined as a time when conditions are favorable for growth; a time when fruit begins to emerge, and a time when challenges are encountered but perseverance prevails. In the Mid-Atlantic region, this season is usually known as summer. Participants were once again encouraged to use the picture as a stimulus for discussion; it should be noted that since two of the groups met in the colder seasons, the picture prompts gave a point of reference when the outside landscape did not.

Descriptors used by the participants for the *growing* season included: excitement, green, beauty, fresh start, transitions, hope, tired, tentative, the need for attention and care, and challenges of wind, rain, frost, weeds, and pests to the emerging plants. For the local church, the growing season manifests in different ways.

Prospect experienced a season with children of different ages and the feeling that the church was a beacon where young ones, if only for a time, could be fed the Good News and sent back out into the world.

For Zoar, Rogation Sunday came to mind when the growth of the earth and God our Creator was given focus; the church also noted that in the *growing* season you see it all because some don't want the change while others welcomed the changes, and inevitably there were bugs that got in and you had to deal with that.

For Concord, the *growing* season was most pronounced in the late 1990s when the church procured its own pastor and no longer shared a pastor with two other churches. It was a time of excitement, determination, and hard work.

For Wesley, seeing newcomers and adapting to new situations also brought about disagreements like insects that come and "you have to deal with it, or it ruins the crop".

One man in the Wesley study also made this observation: Every five years, apple orchards are cut down. New trees are planted to bring about the best fruit. Then it takes a few more years to see the yield of fruit. But the interesting thing is that you need more than one apple tree for the pollination process to work. The fruit depends on pollination; it's not a solo endeavor. The same can be said of the church; it's never been a solo endeavor.

As the third session focused on the *growing* season progressed, the story-linking process brought in the scriptural references of Matthew 13: 24–30 parable of the Wheat and the Weeds, Matthew 13:31–32 parable of the Mustard Seed, and Luke 13:6–9 parable of the fig tree that didn't yield. The 1 Corinthians 3:6–9 passage regarding Paul, Apollos, and God's role in growth was also included. In smaller breakout groups or pairs, the participants read the scripture and discussed what was going on in the story, the characters in the story and how the descriptors for the *growing* season could be seen in the story. Within this dialogue, links between

72

the descriptors, the everyday story, and the biblical story were being made. From the biblical stories, the participants gleaned the following insight:

- We love all and let Jesus do the weeding or we could damage the good.
- The mustard seed plant not only grew bigger than expected but served others in a way that wasn't planned.
- God's timing is not our timing when it comes to growth.
- We are called to be good stewards and let God grow the fruit.
- If we don't see growth, we can't give up but need to try again, maybe make changes, fertilize, do something different or just wait because sometimes it's just a timing issue.
- Remember that God is in the middle of it all for God is Creator of all and giver of life, not us.

The next step of linking with the agricultural-based narrative involved a narrative taken from a farming blog that talks about the frustrations in the *growing* season and the need to work in faith. Faithful and fruitful were the themes that resonated with all of the groups. When asked to reflect on the overarching message and the ways we are called to live faithfully in the *growing* season, one participant noted, "in the growing season you have to trust and have faith that God does His part; He is our rain and our sun and no matter how bad it looks, it's not as bad as it seems. Thank God, we don't need to have spiritual green thumbs to receive His blessings".

Session five brought the groups to the final season, the *harvest* season. Once again, I employed artwork of Vincent Van Gogh, this time his 1888 painting of *Harvest* and used *visio divina* for centering and prayer. From an agricultural perspective, the harvest season is defined as revolving around the product of the land and the work of the Lord to bring it to completion. Participants were asked to reflect on what they see, hear, and feel—physically, emotionally, and spiritually— in the harvest season.

Descriptors of the *harvest* season were as follows: smell of cut hay, reward for hard work, goodness of God, being ripe and ready, different colors, sharing of farm equipment and machinery, sharing with others, sense of community, busyness, a sense of completion and ending. When talking about the local experience of the *harvest* season, one specific story from Prospect emerged that connected the community and the church, as a woman shared the following narrative:

> I remember the threshing machines going from house to house and it was often scheduled so it would be lunch time when they stopped at our house. That was the days when we were tenant farmers next door to the church. It was a time when farmers worked together. I remember we didn't get sodas that often but when it was harvest time, they had a milk cooler and would keep sodas in it. So, when all the work was finished, we could go get one. You can still tell when its harvest season here at the church—it's hard to get in the front door for all the tomatoes and vegetables people have brought in. It was and still is a "take what you need" kind of offering.

In taking the descriptors of the *harvest* season and linking them with the story of the local church, participants were asked to share a time they saw said descriptors within their church's life story. Many noted times when work toward a specific project was completed or a new ministry focus brought in new faces and needed dollars. Hard work, God's provision, and community effort were predominant themes, with a nod given to the inconvenience that was necessary to bring the work together.

Scriptures employed for the biblical link included Ruth 2:1–12 and Luke 12:13–21. From the Ruth passage, participants once again echoed the presence of community and provision as themes in the harvest season. Note was given to the roles of the different people mentioned in the Ruth passage and how it relates to the diverse community that is supposed to make up the church. Also noted was the concept that there was work for everyone to do. In the Luke passage, which was Jesus' parable about the farmer with bigger barns, the participants saw it as a caution in the harvest season. Participants gave similar responses that the farmer in the story had selfish motives and focused on trivial things in life. Many came to the conclusion that they cannot see the harvest in the church for what they get out of it, but must see it as an investment in God's plan for unseen days ahead, all through the lens of "by His grace, and for His glory". Just as in the parable, we need to be careful not to miss opportunities to yield more for the kingdom.

With the *harvest* season in mind, the agricultural narrative for this section dealt with a farming community's response to a fatal farming accident and the need to bring in the crop. While the story shared happened in recent years, study participants began sharing stories they had experienced and heard over the years about farming accidents and how the farming community always came together to give emotional and physical support to the family or group in need. The discussion grew into the overarching theme of different jobs and different people for one purpose, much like the varied gifts for the one body in one spirit for one Lord.

The general consensus of all the groups was that God was in all parts of the harvest season, from the growth into fullness to the sharing of the fruit into the community. They also concluded that to realize the harvest in their own church would take more contemplation.

One more session was offered as a concluding session for the study groups. In this session, the image given to ponder was a saying by Doe Zantamata: "What you see depends on how you see the world; to most people, this is just dirt. To a farmer, it is potential". With the idea farming entails a plan and process, participants were encouraged to reflect on the idea that all seasons are cyclical in nature and thereby of equal importance to health and growth of the crops, as well as the church. The question was posed: at the church, how do we plan with "the end in mind" when it comes to being God's farm? This question then led to the question, "If we are God's farm for a purpose, what does scripture say about our purpose as the church?"

Scripture was once again used to help guide discussion, using Galatians 6:7–10, 2 Corinthians 5:17, and Colossians 3:23. Echoes of the Great Commission and Great Commandment were heard across the group responses, along with reminders like: remember to be thankful and prayerful in all circumstances, we need to plant in order to reap what is sown, do good to all people, don't give up, don't be discouraged, don't grow weary, and you are the only Jesus some people will see. With that said, an example of Hope Presbyterian Church from Kathleen Norris' book, *Dakota*, was offered as the power of community within a small church to the glory going to God.

Small rural churches are important because they are located in rural communities that need the gospel lived out in real and relevant ways. While these small churches may seem insignificant in the twenty-first-century culture around us, God assures us we are called according to God's purpose and plan no matter our size.

Through the study that raised up the stories of the individuals and their plot on God's Farm known as the church, I was able to truly listen and see the lay of the land and move to the second step of acknowledgment and addressing that current situation.

N: Need to Work the Land

"Therefore, my dear friends, as you have always obeyed—not only in my presence, but now much more in my absence—continue to work out your salvation with fear and trembling" (Philippians 2:12 NIV).

Farming is a combination of good land stewardship and good investment of resources. In flat terrain like southern Delaware, growers find the environment perfect for raising chickens in long chicken houses. With more local chickens, more local grain is needed. Hay, soybeans, and various vegetables benefit local farmers with additional goods for sale. Additionally, if one area of the field is prone to flood, the farmer takes that into account when planting and planning for the harvest.

The twenty-first-century church is a consumer-driven church that must know the needs of its surrounding

community in order to be relevant. Churches often "want"

more people and more revenue but "need" to be rooted in

spiritual disciplines, so the growth comes from God. Small

rural churches can be strategically located to know and

meet the needs face-to-face, especially when poverty is

higher in rural areas than in many urban areas due to lack of

transportation and jobs and limited health care services. What

isn't limited in rural areas are opportunities to bring the hope

and life in Jesus Christ to others face-to-face.

Through listening and learning about the lay of the

land in reference to the church's current physical location,

and then refining the listening and sharing process to assess

and acknowledge the current situation, the time comes when

hands need to get into the ground and work the land. And the

work of the land may be similar to others but is unique to its

grounded identity in Christ by its location, experiences, and

spiritual health.

While most churches often "want" more people in the

pews and dollars in the bank, the need must be one grounded

in the Great Commandment and the Great Commission. To

love God first and foremost is the only way the church can

love and genuinely be in ministry to others. And it is a love that has to be put into action within and outside of the church walls. Increased volume of fruit from the farm does no good if it lacks the goodness from being borne of healthy earth and plants.

At Wesley, the face-to-face "need" includes single parent families, grandparents raising grandchildren, the face of one who knows the struggle with addiction and has learned there is strength in community, and the increase in migrant workers becoming permanent fixtures in community. To meet the need is to claim the spiritual mandate to love God and love neighbor. Ways that Wesley has extended its ministry to the community has been to provide Spanish translation for signage and room rental agreements, to offer summer brown bag lunches to a large number of children who get free lunches during the school year, to place video screens with closed captioning in the sanctuary to help those who are hearing impaired follow the worship service, and to make handicap accessible entrances to the church that benefit the elderly and parents with young children.

In 2014, the church was still in a fallow season but discussion and planning on how to be faithful in the current season was initiated. With an aging facility and sagging

finances, the church decided to step out in faith. After forty

days of focused prayer, the trustees presented a three-year,

three-stage Capital Improvement Campaign (CIC), estimated

to cost over $300,000. The project included replacement of

a sixty-year old boiler used to heat the church, restoration

of restroom facilities, installation of handicap accessible

entrances within and outside of the building, lighting and

electrical updates, repair of flooring, replacement of carpet,

and installation of signage and needed technology throughout

the building. Undertaking the project would mean relying

on God and not just individuals in the church to make the

project completion a reality. While some were tentative, the

decision was made to take on the first stage of the project

on the Sunday that the heat went out in the nursery and the

sanctuary.

The year 2015 saw the first phase of the CIC project

completed ahead of schedule and paid in full; to this step,

the church gave witness and praise to what God had done for

God's glory. Discussion began concerning what ministries to

keep, which ones to expand, and which ones to plant anew. A

growing interest in prayer began adding nutrient to the soil of

God's farm plot at Wesley.

In 2016, the soil of the church was literally and figuratively turned over as the restroom phase or stage two of the CIC project began. The second stage brought the most expense and the most inconvenience to the people, and yet again the project was completed before the end of the year and paid in full. For the first two years, it should be noted that no money was borrowed from the bank to meet expenditures. And the step of faith had yielded a bonus crop for the budget ended the year in the black for the first time in recent years.

In the growing season of 2017, the CIC project was completed ahead of schedule with the help of funds from a line of credit; however, by February 2018, the line of credit was also paid in full. The fall of 2017 saw a re-dedication of the building to the glory of God, for God's plan and God's purposes. It was also in this growing season that another interesting event happened; one that didn't gain much attention at the time.

In spring 2017, I was led to walk around the property across the street, an acre within town limits that had forty-two paved parking spaces, a grassy area, and a vacant building. I didn't know why at the time, but I prayed for

God's will to be done on this land and for the church to hear

God's call to action in God's timing. As I walked around that

lot, I heard the Spirit say, "Call on me, the owner of cattle

on a thousand hills, claim this land for you are to expand

your mission into the community". After that prayer walk, I

went back across the street, walked into my office, and wrote

those words in my journal. When our district prayer journal

requested prayers for individual churches to be prayed over

during the year, I included the words I had heard into that

district prayer journal on behalf of Wesley.

Fast forwarding to February 2018, I received a call

from the trustee chair and God gave the next spiritual marker.

He told me that the owner of the property across the street

was selling the property. The owner had not listed it yet

and wanted to let the church know since our only parking

availability was the street surrounding the church and the

good graces of said property owner across the street. I had to

smile because God once again showed his people promised

land and the people had an opportunity to step out in faith.

Wesley was able to find the financing and as of June 2018, for

the first time in the church's history, the church has its own parking lot for attending services and events at the church.

God had just given us more land on which to plant and grow.

As the *growing* season continued into 2018, and we
continued prayers for God to bring more people, we saw
God work in another unexpected way. Bethesda, a very small
church of a couple dozen people on the edge of Georgetown,
was struggling and would be partnered with Wesley to create
a new circuit. While as an elder in the United Methodist
church I was to be appointed full time, the past two years
I had volunteered to serve with three-fourths time pay so
the church would not focus on money but focus on what
God was doing. The partnering with Bethesda allowed me
to return to full time, allowed Wesley some breathing room
with its finances, and gave Bethesda a full-time pastor and a
sister church to walk alongside her. While Bethesda ended
up running out of funds within the year, and subsequently
closing their doors, growth was seen in new ways as the
Bethesda membership was replanted elsewhere to continue
their growth.

Meanwhile, within Wesley, other growth could be
seen. New ministries started cropping up. Where once there
was no prayer team, a prayer team had grown to six regular

members who often had others stop by on Tuesday evenings to be prayed for or to pray with the group; the prayer team now also initiated regular prayer focuses throughout the year and participates visibly in each Sunday worship service. The youth group that had died off was reborn with as many as ten at a weekend youth group meeting. Reliance on prayer and God's provision took on a whole new light as the landscape and health of the church began to change for the good.

Upon my arrival, Wesley was a church with two services: a 9:00 a.m. contemporary service held in the community hall and an 11:00 a.m. traditional service held in the sanctuary. Congregants at the two services had become polarized to a certain extent; at times it seemed like two churches in one building. In winter 2017, attendance at both services was making it difficult to secure two tech teams, two worship leaders, ushers, and other positions for each of the services. The church leadership decided to create a new single service to diminish the burnout and polarization on Memorial Day Sunday, 2018.

Change has not been easy because the land has been turned upside down. Some want to return to the status quo. Others want to move faster in changes. A few people have chosen not to come to worship because they disagree with the land purchase, the change in worship time, and format, or that some of the new members are not "like them". Turning over soil is not just used to plant but also to pull up weeds from choking out new growth. However, as the parable tells us, sometimes we need to let the weeds and the wheat grow together and let God do the sorting in the appropriate time.

Cultural change has deep roots and the process of farming God's tract called Wesley will be an ongoing process over the years. The sharing of stories proved a way to open dialogue and possibilities, encouraging the church to tend to the land in all seasons while encouraging the good that comes from diversifying our efforts across the life of the church. The introduction and re-introduction of agrarian-based narratives planted new seeds and reconnected people to the biblical narrative and to the reality of where God has planted them in this life and on this land they call home.

For with change in season, diversity becomes the important fourth step to healthy growth on God's farm.

.

D: Diversity in the Fieldwork

There is one body, but it has many parts. But all its many parts make up one body. It is the same with Christ. We were all baptized by one Holy Spirit. And so we are formed into one body. It didn't matter whether we were Jews or Gentiles, slaves or free people. We were all given the same Spirit to drink. So the body is not made up of just one part. It has many parts. 1 Corinthians 12:12–14 (NIR)V

Just as a local dairy has multiple flavors of ice cream to draw people to its farm, people enter church through more than one door and for more than one reason. The farm and the small church must share the goal to not just survive but to thrive. Any farmer knows that diversification is necessary to survive in the twenty-first century. While the gospel doesn't change, the small rural church's re-presenting of Christ to the community will make the difference in a living church or just existing one. From the previous steps in the spiritual cultivation process for the small rural church, strengths of the specific community of faith will be unearthed. Pairing congregational and community strengths with the power and perspective that God owns the church and God alone brings the growth creates fertile soil. The next steps in growing spiritual fruit are for both to have the courage to be different.

In turning over new ground for spiritual growth, Wesley planted seeds of hope and health in familiar ways and in new ways. Mission projects which were once limited to the adult members are now undertaken by the children three times a year. A once empty youth classroom is now the center of activity for intentional faith formation and launching zone for "being the hands and feet of Christ". Not all attempts to bring diversity into familiar territory are met with welcome; as cultivation turns over ground, the process is often messy, stinky, and worms often surface. But when worms can be seen aerating the ground, something new is ready to emerge.

To address the need for diversity in the landscape where one is located, three approaches prove helpful in discerning next steps: Mission, Action, and Prayer.

Diversity and ministry can be seen in engaging

with mission opportunities at the local, regional, and global

level. For Wesley, this meant that locally the men's group

supported the Native American community by providing

parking assistance for their annual powwow, regionally the

entire church collected items and funds for flood victims

in the southern area of the United States, and with a global

perspective, the children, youth, and women's group made

dresses for girls in Africa. Mission diversity should include

a variety of encounters, not just sending a check. Personal

interaction with a missionary or first-hand experience in

the process of helping builds relationships within diverse

missional opportunities. When relationships emerge, both the

receiver and the giver see the life-giving reality of the gospel.

Diversity and action are essential to build relationships. Just

as farming communities will often gather to support one

another in times of need, like helping bring in the crops for a

fellow farmer with cancer, cooperation and action result from

coming alongside one another. Too often, if the church keeps

an arm's length from those they are seeking to serve, an "us

and them" dynamic can form and opportunities for blessings

can be missed. To accomplish diversity in action, Wesley

engaged some of the Boy Scouts they hosted in a Bible-based study that resulted in a scout badge and having a financially supported missionary come and speak to the congregation. However, other areas needed action to move simply from diversity being present to inclusion becoming part of the church's DNA. Relationships that include and not just identify differences can add layers of richness to the church's soil for growing kingdom fruit.

One area of diversity moving into a more relationship-based inclusion can be seen in ministry to and with people with disabilities. Historically, the church has welcomed people with disabilities to taste and see that the Lord is good, but have not included them to the level to which they were asked to take part in the preparation, planting, and harvesting of the land. With the passage of the Americans with Disabilities Act in 1990, the cry of "nothing for us without us" could be heard in the halls of legislature and should be echoed in the halls of our churches. By expanding the diversity of local church action in mission from merely identifying people with needs to seeing the unique gifts, talents, and perspectives offered, gospel seeds can grow deeper roots.

Finally, diversity and prayer are the fertilizer for the crops we plan to grow for the kingdom. Personal prayer, corporate prayer, and focused prayer and fasting in certain seasons are all needed to not only discern next steps but to saturate the ground with trust in God who is ever faithful. As the Apostle Paul writes, Creator God is the only One who can bring growth (1 Corinthians 3:6–9 NCV)

It should be noted that diversity leading to inclusion is only possible as the type of soil in the church will allow. Change for change's sake does not necessarily transform but diversifying our efforts to include building relationships with the land and the people of the land, create an environment where blessings are both given and received. To be transformed by the diversity on God's farm, ministry and mission must be included within our hearts and our lives for that is where the transforming power of Christ brings new life. Looking beyond what we have always done to what could we do is what gives us vision, focus, and momentum to turn over new ground and begin planting new seeds.

REBECCA COLLISON

LOOKING ACROSS THE HORIZON

"See, I am doing a new thing! Now, it springs up; do you not perceive it? I am making a way in the wilderness and streams in the wasteland". (Isaiah 43:19 NIV)

Is Apollos important? No! Is Paul important? No! We are only servants of God who helped you believe. Each one of us did the work God gave us to do. I planted the seed, and Apollos watered it. But God is the One who made it grow. We are God's workers, working together; you are like God's farm...(1 Corinthians 3:5–6, 9 NCV)

The LAND process, outlined in the last three chapters, with its spiritual grounding in our stories, has helped Wesley and some other churches to cultivate spirituality amid cultural changes in order to bring hope and health to its small rural context. Like many processes, it is not easy, and it is a work not quickly finished. Small and rural-based churches remain a people, a parcel of holy ground, whose ground must continually be worked and assessed to ensure it is yielding fruit, for that is the purpose of being God's field or farm.

Mainline denominations, like the struggling United Methodist Church, once offered local churches an identity in the religious landscape of America but now create an unsettled tension and loss of stability. One course of action for local churches, especially small and rural-based churches, is going back to the land from whence we came to re-ground ourselves in the identity of the eternal and life-giving God. As we work on our identity as a church, a plot of God's farm, we look at the seasons we have been through, realizing that change like the seasons is inevitable and will always bring challenges and celebrations when we remain faithful where God has planted us. Our role is to prepare the land faithfully and appropriately for each changing season we face.

Ecclesiastes 3:1 reminds us "to everything there is a season, and a time to every purpose under heaven". Those words are true for the land of the farmer and of our faith, especially those whose faith sprouted in small rural churches. In 1925, a concern emerged for young people who were losing interest and leaving the farm; out of that concern, the

Future Farmers of America (FFA) was born from thirty-three

students in eighteen states. Today, even with farming seen in

a decline, all fifty states are currently chartered members with

a mission to prepare future generations for the challenges of

feeding a growing population.[82] At the 1978 FFA Convention,

broadcast journalist Paul Harvey offered the address, "And

God Made a Farmer". Over the years, the National Farm

Bureau began its Sunday convention session with the hymn,

"Great is Thy Faithfulness", whose second verse was a

reminder:

> Summer and winter and springtime and harvest;
>
> Sun, moon and stars in their courses above,
>
> Join with all nature in manifold witness
>
> To thy great faithfulness, mercy and love.[83]

And over the seasons, perspectives and centers

of focus change. Currently, the National Farm Bureau no

longer includes the God-praising hymn at opening of the

Sunday session at their annual convention. Yet, the FFA

Creed of the agricultural based student organization still

states the following hope within its creed: "I believe in the future of farming with a faith born not of words but deeds... the promise of better days through better ways, even as the better things we now enjoy come to us from the struggles of former years".[84] Likewise, the practices in our churches have changed, but our creedal foundation remains a true layer of the rich soil that brings life to our communities of faith.

Several decades have passed since broadcast journalist Paul Harvey offered words of encouragement to future farmers eager to show what they could do with the land. The number of churches, specifically rural churches has diminished since that time, but their demise is greatly exaggerated. As long as people need to eat, the farmers will be needed to work the land. And if there are folks living inside and outside of the city centers trying to find their way in the world, churches in all locations, including small rural churches will be needed to spiritually feed the hungry with sustenance that only comes from the Creator of the Land.

In a recent study by Thom Rainer, an increase of attention and importance is being given to rural and small churches. Rainer notes the reasons are varied including a re-newed commitment to neighborhood churches and the value of community.[85] The challenge of the small rural churches is to be alive and not just exist, recognizing the demands of the current culture while ultimately standing on the truth that God's ways are not always humankind's ways.

So, in the style of Harvey's FFA address, I conclude with words of encouragement infused with God's Spirit to the small rural churches seeking to thrive in the twenty-first century in search of hope and health. It is not a word soaked in sentimentality, but the strength of relationship and life found on God's farm:

> And on the eighth day, God looked down on his creation and said, "I need to pull a special group of people for a special mission in this world".
>
> So, God raised up the small rural church.
>
> God said, "I need some folks willing to meet out in the middle of nowhere with no phone signal found, a gathering place where they can talk about weather and politics and religion, and still work shoulder-to-shoulder to build me a house of prayer".
>
> So, God raised up the small rural church.

"I need some folks who sing together, pray together, share, care, and dare together and sit down to a meal like family, and even if someone sits on their pew, they can still say 'I love you brother, I love you sister'...and mean it".

So, God raised up the small rural church.

God said, "I need some folks who are willing to let the worker come into the church without taking off his boots even though covered with mud, to let the farmer miss the trustee meeting because there are beans to get in before the rain, to let the sister sing off key and not kick her out of the choir because all can make a joyful noise, to let the babies cry and the toddlers whine during the service because it is a sign of life, and still have time to comfort the older confused member who can't remember the words any more but joins in with an "amen" at the end of each prayer".So, God raised up the small rural church.

God had to have some people willing to travel in the cold and heat, and summer and winter, and day and night, by foot, by bike, by horse, or by whatever means necessary whenever the church doors are open just to worship the almighty, all-knowing, all-powerful Creator God who has given them breath for that very day and very purpose

So, God raised up the small rural church.

God said, "I need some folks who believe I exist in places where two or three are gathered in my name, where the bank account is small but hearts are big, and where 'all lives matter' is not a political statement but a way of life".

It had to be a group of people who were willing to work hard for the kingdom of God where they are planted—at the crossroads and in the fields and forests and on the sweeping plains across the land, equipped with and thankful for what they have, and who were willing to let God be God; a group of people who realize things of this earth are temporary but life in the Maker of Heaven and Earth is forever, and so they are willing to share, as the generations before them had done, the importance of faith and their messy but grace-filled role in growing fruit for God's farm—So, God raised up the small rural

church. Thanks be to God.

APPENDIX

God's Farm Study by Rebecca Kelly Collison

Session 1: The Land

Experience

In the movie, "Gone with the Wind" (1939), landowner and farmer Gerald O'Hara reminds his daughter Scarlett that she is an heir to the family plantation named Tara and that land is important to her identity and future. He says:

Do you mean to tell me...that land doesn't mean anything to you? Why land is the only thing in the world worth workin' for, worth fightin' for, worth dyin' for, because it's the only thing that lasts.

- What is your experience with the word "heir"?
- Do you have something in your life you hope to

pass down for generations to come?

- The word "land" brings varied images, feelings, experience. List words that describe your experience with land (e.g. what it looks like, what it feels like, what it reminds you of).

- O'Hara sees land as being important because "it's the only thing that lasts". This concept is one commonly found in farming communities. Why might this concept of "heir" and "land" be important to the church in the twenty-first century?

Explore

Land is important. God formed us of land. For that reason, we are connected to the land in a physical and spiritual way.

"The LORD God took a handful of soil and made a man. God breathed life into the man, and the man started breathing" (Genesis 2:7 CEV).

From being formed in the Garden of Eden, to Noah's finding a place to land after the flood, to Abraham's leaving of his land of origin, to Joshua ushering a new era in the Promised Land, the role of land has always been key in the lives of God's people in the Old Testament. But it is more than just geography. Jesus, who was born in a farm structure, told ten parables directly connecting the people to farming references.

Identity through connection is important. Author Ellen F. Davis in her book *Scripture, Culture, and Agriculture* noted this connection understood by those who stay close to the land. She writes:

> Agrarians know the land, not as an inert object, but as a fellow creature that can justly expect something from us whose lives depend on it..."And YHWH God formed the human being ['adam], dust from the fertile soil ['adama]" (Genesis 2:7). Although the wordplay is captured surprisingly well by the English pun "human from humus", the Hebrew is more fully descriptive of their family resemblance...it evokes the specific relationship between a people and their particular place.

As a farmer, the character Gerald O'Hara in the movie, knew that everyone needs a place of grounding that confirms their identity and their future. For Christians, and for the Church, that land is Christ.

Our role as God's farm is important. Witness Lee once wrote in the *Purpose of God's Purpose by Christ's Fulfillment in us*, "A farm is a plot of land for growing things. The church is God's land to grow Christ, not in an individual way, but in a corporate way...something of Christ will be grown up in each of us".

As Paul writes in 1 Corinthians 3:9 *"you are God's cultivated field [His garden, His vineyard]"*. We are God's farm and it is from the land that we can gain not only identity, but also direction on how to bear fruit for the Lord.

Engage

As followers of Christ, we can find our way through the spiritual geography of our individual lives and of the life of our church as we reclaim the importance of the land in our lives.

- Share a story about a time when you needed to get away and you went to "the land" to find your grounding. Explain what prompted you to go, where you went, and what was the result of your "getting away to the land".

- Share the story how your church came to be on the location that it currently exists. Why would location be important for a community of faith to be grounded?

In the Bible, locations such as Hebron, Bethel, Mt. Horeb, and the River Jordan all have a significance in the identity of a people by their experience of God in that place.

- What specific place or location holds spiritual significance for you and why?

Extend

Diana Butler Bass writes in *Grounded: Finding God in the World—A Spiritual Revolution:*

God is the ground, the grounding, that which grounds us. We experience this when we understand that soil is holy, water gives life, the sky opens the imagination, our roots matter, home is a divine place, and our lives are linked with our neighbors' and with those around the globe. This world, not heaven, is the sacred stage of our times. (pg. 26)

In our lives and in our churches, we go through seasons

similar to the seasons of the land. The seasons are as follows:

The Fallow Season: when the climate and the land are not conducive to widespread planting in the natural outdoors. As such, planting and growing are at a standstill; this may look like the winter season of empty fields.

The Planting Season: when the climate and the land are ready to be prepared to receive seed and new plantings; this may look like the spring season with overturned soil and seeds going in the ground.

The Growing Season: When the climate and the land have received the seed and the growing process is underway; this may look like the summer season with growth coming from the seed and maturing into the desired crop.

The Harvest Season: when the growing is completed, and the finished crop is taken out of the field to be dispersed in various ways; this may look like the fall season when crops are brought in and the harvest celebrated.

In looking at the seasons above, which season best represents the current season of your life? The current season of your church's life?

Gleanings from Lesson One

During the week, it is helpful to go back and review the lesson. It is not required but sometimes sitting with scripture and stories can help us grow spiritually. If there are any questions you didn't answer during the session, now may be a time to sit with the question to seek the answer that comes to you.

You are encouraged to journal, writing down your thoughts or stories that come to mind, or to write prayers specific to the season you just discussed. Either way, spend some time re-visiting this season as a personal reflection for yourself and your church.

Day One: What words currently describe my spiritual life?

Day Two: If I could imagine a landscape that reflects my spiritual life, what would it look like? Describe it.

Day Three: What words currently describe my church's spiritual life?

Day Four: Imagine a physical landscape that reflects your

church's spiritual life. What would it look like? Describe it.

Day Five: What words or prayer would you like to say to God about the current spiritual condition around yourself? What questions do you have? What praises do you have?

SESSION 2: THE FALLOW SEASON

Experience

From an agrarian perspective, the fallow season is when fields are bare and nothing seems to be growing. For many, this season is experienced as the season known as winter. In looking out over the fields in the winter or fallow season, what do you see and hear? What do you feel physically, emotionally, and spiritually?

Explore the Everyday Story

The following compilation of comments reflects how one church felt the fallow season in this way:

My church has been experiencing a fallow season for probably ten to fifteen years, due to decline in the number of people attending worship services, Sunday school, Bible study, and youth group. I grieve for the time when all of these activities were full of people. We say, "I remember when . . ". We say, "Someone needs to step up and do . . ". and, "The younger people should be taking on the responsibilities". We all have different opinions on what is wrong or why nothing much seems to be growing, or why younger families do not participate in the life of the church.

We have talked some about what we should do to grow our church attendance, focusing on what we think should happen and without focusing on what God would have us do. We do not, usually, make or carry out plans. We do not often talk about how we can reach out to others in love, in Jesus' name.

I don't think we all love whoever walks through our doors. And that goes for the newcomers and some who have been here a while. It feels like there is a lot of lack of communication, conflict over situations and lack of a spirit of love among members.

Those empty spaces in the pews feel cold and lonely, hard—even with their cushioning. There are times this season seems long and unending.

- How does this story echo the descriptive words you used under your "experience" of the fallow season?

- Share an example of how your church felt during a fallow season.

Engage the Biblical Story

Read the following passages and reflect on who is involved, what is going on and why?

- Exodus 23:11–12

- Jeremiah 32:1–25

- Habakkuk 3:17–19

How are the characteristics we listed for the fallow season seen in these passages?

Story Linking Process

Take the descriptions given in the Experience section and compare with reflections on the everyday story. Then compare and link with the biblical story. Use guiding questions below.

What similarities and feelings resonate with the biblical story and the everyday story?

115

Where is God in the fallow season as seen in the everyday story and the biblical narratives?

Extend the Agricultural Narrative

Read the following and discuss this excerpt from Julie Peter's Spirituality and Health blog, "The Fallow Field: The Virtue of Doing Nothing"

> *We live in a world that privileges work, productivity, and speed, so when I take the time to do nothing in particular, I feel guilty. I am not carpe-ing any diems here. So why do I feel such a strong need to sit on my couch and watch TV shows from the early nineties?*
>
> *I think it's for the same reason growing fields need to sometimes lie fallow. Farmers will occasionally plough a field that normally grows a crop like corn or wheat, and simply not seed it for that growing season. The blank, unseeded space is a "fallow field".*
>
> *During this time of apparently nothing, the soil is regenerating, and restoring its fertility so that by next season it will be ready to grow. The farmers don't treat the soil, inject it with fertilizers, plant better seeds, or*

poke at it with a magic wand. They just get out of the way.

We are a culture of human doings, not human beings. We are not in the habit of taking time off to let the body and mind do their mysterious internal work...It's hard to trust that just because you can't see growth or changes doesn't mean it isn't happening.

Giving my instincts a chance to talk to me passively can be helpful. Sometimes it's also a little scary: if I give myself the space to think and feel properly, I might discover that I need to change something...Trust your fallow field, and it will be ready when the growing season comes.

Highlight the parts of this story that connect to descriptors of the Fallow Season and to other parts of the everyday story and biblical story. Then use the story linking process to continue to make connections between all four sections. *If time to explore the questions below, do so in small groups. If no time remains, encourage participants to explore these questions, write down their thoughts, and bring them to the next session.*

- What message seems to emerge for your individual life and for the life of a congregation?

- What is a way God calls us to live faithfully in the Fallow Season?

Gleanings from Lesson Two

During the week, it is helpful to go back and review the lesson. It is not required but sometimes sitting with scripture and stories can help us grow spiritually. If there are any questions you didn't answer during the session, now may be a time to sit with the question to seek the answer that comes to you.

You are encouraged to journal, writing down your thoughts or stories that come to mind, or to write prayers specific to the season you just discussed. Either way, spend some time re-visiting this season as a personal reflection for yourself and your church.

Day One: What was the most important thing I learned about myself and the fallow season?

Day Two: What was the most important thing I learned about my church and the fallow season?

Day Three: What do I see as the greatest challenge of the

fallow season?

Day Four: What do I see as the greatest opportunity in the fallow season?

Day Five: What words or prayer would you like to say to God about the fallow season? What questions do you have? What praises do you have?

Session 3: The Planting Season

Experience

From an agricultural perspective, the planting season is when ground is turned over to make room for a new planting and plans are put into motion to fertilize and nurture the new growth emerging. In the planting season, a farmer must often cultivate - pull up and turn over - the soil by reshaping it so it can accept the seed and water needed to grow. Imagine looking out over the fields in the planting season, what do you see and hear? What do you feel - physically, emotionally, and spiritually?

Explore the Everyday Story

One church felt the planting season in this way:

The planting season at our church was when we decided to put new life in our congregation. We began planting seeds by having sermons and studies about what it meant to be a disciple because I think some of us had been doing it (church) so long, we had forgotten...We started looking for ways to plant seeds outside of the church, beginning with collecting change for missions and then looking for events happening in town that we could be a part of. That took getting over some attitudes and preconceptions we had – but it was breaking new ground, a kind of turning over ground so we could plant more seeds...You can't plant seeds if you stay within the walls of the church...you can do the planning and preparing there, but you also have to go outside.

How does this story echo the descriptive words you used under your "experience" of the planting season? Share an example of how your church felt during a planting season.

Engage the Biblical Story

Read Mark 4:3–9, 13–20. Who is in the story and what is going on?

Read John 12:24. How are the characteristics we listed for the planting season seen in these passages?

Story Linking Process.

Take the descriptions given in the Experience section and compare with reflections on the everyday story. Then compare and link with the biblical story. Use guiding questions below

What similarities and feelings resonate with the biblical story and the everyday story?

Where is God in the planting season as seen in the everyday story and the biblical narratives?

Extend the Agricultural Narrative

Read the following in pairs then discuss this excerpt from Noah Sanders book *Born Again Dirt*:

One of my older Christian neighbors was once approached by an extension agent who asked, "Mr. Hay, I have noticed that every year you have a beautiful garden. What is your secret?" My neighbor replied in his deep, dignified southern accent, "Well, first we work hard to prepare the soil for planting. Then we look in the almanac to see what day would be good for planting according to the moon, for the Bible says the moon was created to mark the times and seasons. And after we get everything in the ground, I go sit on the log over by the side of the garden, take off my hat, and pray, "Lord, we've done the best we know how. Now it is up to you to give us a good garden". I don't think that extension agent went around telling Mr. Hay's secret to a good garden, but I think Mr. Hay hit the nail on the head. Our job is to be faithful and the fruit is up to the Lord.

Many of us farmers struggle with worry. When there are so many things out of our control, we tend to worry about whether all our hard work will pay off in the end. However, Christ commands us not to worry. He provides for the birds and the flowers, and He will provide for us if we are faithful to be obedient to Him. When the Lord does bless us, we need to acknowledge that the increase of the land is a gift of God, not an automatic right that we have because of our work. May we never boast save in the Lord". (pp.17–18).

Highlight the parts of this story that connect to descriptors of the planting season and to other parts of the everyday story and biblical story. Then, use the story linking process to continue to make connections between all four sections. If time to explore the questions below, do so in small groups. If no time remains, encourage participants to explore these questions, write down their thoughts, and bring them to the next session.

What message seems to emerge for your individual life and for the life of your congregation? What is a way God calls us to live faithfully in the planting season?

Gleanings from Lesson Three

During the week, it is helpful to go back and review the lesson. It is not required but sometimes sitting with scripture and stories can help us grow spiritually. If there are any questions you didn't answer during the session, now may be a time to sit with the question to seek the answer that comes to you.

In the space below, you are encouraged to journal, writing down your thoughts or stories that come to mind, or to write prayers specific to the season you just discussed. Either way, spend some time revisiting this season as a personal reflection for yourself and your church.

Day One: What was the most important thing I learned about myself and the planting season?

Day Two: What was the most important thing I learned about my church and the planting season?

Day Three: What do I see as the greatest challenge of the planting season?

Day Four: What do I see as the greatest opportunity in the planting season?

Day Five: What words or prayer would you like to say to God about the planting season? What questions do you have? What praises do you have?

SESSION 4: THE GROWING SEASON

Experience

From an agricultural perspective, the growing season is defined as a time when conditions are favorable for growth; a time when fruit begins to emerge, a time when challenges are encountered but perseverance prevails. In looking out over the fields in the growing season, what do you see and hear? What do you feel physically, emotionally, and spiritually?

Explore the Everyday Story

One church felt the growing season in this way:

We went through a growing season within our church when we started to grow in size. We had to adjust the "this is the way we always did it attitude" to a group of people who were coming and had never done church that way. It meant making allowances for children who were not always quiet in service. It meant we needed to put step stools in the restrooms so children could reach the sink; we never had those before. It meant making a ramp so the one person with a walker would have an easier time getting in the building; and don't you know it, then other folks brought friends who had walkers and made use of the ramp. Many of us old timers had to get in the habit of saying our name; instead of thinking everyone already knew it. And we found we started to grow closer as our family grew. Not everyone was happy about the growth and some disagreements crept in. Some folks left. Most folks stayed. In all of it, we tried to keep the main thing the main thing...that was, we were called to be faithful disciples—love God and love others, even others we didn't know—and God would take care of the growth.

How does this story echo the descriptive words you used under your experience of the growing season? Share an example of how your church felt during a growing season.

Engage the Biblical Story

Read Matthew 13:24–30, Matthew 13:31–32, and Luke 13:6–9. Who is in each passage and what is going on? Then read 1 Corinthians 3:6–9. How are the characteristics we listed for the growing season seen in these passages?

Story Linking Process.

Take the descriptions given in the Experience section and compare with reflections on the everyday story. Then compare and link with the biblical story. Use guiding questions below.

What similarities and feelings resonate with the biblical story and the everyday story?

Where is God in the growing season as seen in the everyday story and the biblical narratives?

Extend the Agricultural Narrative

Read the following excerpt from Christine Hoover's blog entitled, *Three Lessons from the Farmer about Faith.*

Farming is backbreaking work, dirty work, detailed work, and, most of all, it is risky work. There aren't any guarantees. A few years ago, Travis reminds me, when the crop stood beautiful and bountiful in the fields, ready for harvest, a hurricane blew through the Rio Grande Valley and wiped it away entirely. All that labor, all that grime, all that waiting, for nothing.

What is the point? Why would we invest everything in a risky venture? We might ask this, thinking of our own lives and our own efforts to produce a spiritual harvest and have seemingly harvested nothing or been wiped out entirely.

The farmer looks at his failed crop as a tangible reminder that the harvest inevitably belongs to the Lord. The farmer must be faithful to lay the groundwork for the harvest, but the harvest cannot be forced; it can only happen through the Lord's providence.

There are things that pop up in the growing season that aren't helpful or what you want to see. We get rain that we don't want on the crops. I've learned not to go look at the crops on the day it rains, because that's when it looks the worst. It's never as bad as we thought after we come through it, though, and even what doesn't look good is working toward the end goal of the harvest. In the end, no matter what the crop looks like, we have to trust God that he's going to take care of us. To focus on fruitfulness is a frustrating endeavor; to work in faith is all we are asked to do. And it's really all we can do.

Highlight the parts of this story that connect to descriptors of the growing season and to other parts of the everyday story and biblical story. Then use the story-linking process to continue to make connections between all four sections. *If time to explore the questions below, do so in small groups. If no time remains, encourage participants to explore these questions, write down their thoughts, and bring them to the next session.*

What message seems to emerge for your individual life and for the life of your congregation? What is a way God calls us to live faithfully in the growing season?

Gleanings from Lesson Four

During the week, it is helpful to go back and review the lesson. It is not required but sometimes sitting with scripture and stories can help us grow spiritually. If there are any questions you didn't answer during the session, now may be a time to sit with the question to seek the answer that comes to you.

On the space below, you are encouraged to journal, writing down your thoughts or stories that come to mind, or to write prayers specific to the season you just discussed. Either way, spend some time re-visiting this season as a personal reflection for yourself and your church.

Day One: What was the most important thing I learned about myself and the growing season?

Day Two: What was the most important thing I learned about my church and the growing season?

Day Three: What do I see as the greatest challenge of the growing season?

Day Four: What do I see as the greatest opportunity in the growing season?

Day Five: What words or prayer would you like to say to God about the growing season? What questions do you have? What praises do you have?

Session 5: The Harvest Season

Experience

From an agricultural perspective, the harvest season is defined as a time when the product and the work have come to a completion. Imagine looking out over the fields in the harvest season, what do you see and hear? What do you feel physically, emotionally, and spiritually?

Explore the Everyday Story

One church felt the harvest season in this way:

It had taken three years of planning, preparing, tearing down, building up, and raising funds for it all to come together, but it finally did. Our Capital Improvement Campaign was complete. We had begun with a prayer asking God to provide and we ended giving God the glory for His provision. Our restoration and renovation project began with just a trickle of donations, but then more and more hands helped out. Some pulled out old flooring and plumbing. Others put new carpet and bathroom fixtures. All were inconvenienced at some point, but it was worth it in the end. It wasn't easy, but together we collected over $200,000 without incurring debt and enlisted hundreds of man hours. The new improvements helped us financially give more to mission and be more effective in our mission and ministry as the church. And it was all God. We can't boast about it because God did what we couldn't. All the praise goes to God.

How does this story echo the descriptive words you used under your "experience" of the harvest season? Share an example of how your church felt during a harvest season.

Engage the Biblical Story

Read Ruth 2:1–12 and Luke 12:13–21. Who is in each passage and what is going on? Then re-visit 1 Corinthians 3:6–9. How are the characteristics we listed for the harvest season seen in these passages?

Story Linking Process.

Take the descriptions given in the Experience section and compare with reflections on the everyday story. Then compare and link with the biblical story. Use guiding questions below.

What similarities and feelings resonate with the biblical story and the everyday story?

Where is God in the harvest season as seen in the everyday story and the biblical narratives?

Extend the Agricultural Narrative

Read the following in pairs then discuss the July 11, 2016 news story broadcast by WBOC News in Salisbury, Maryland, titled "Farming community rallies behind killed Parsonsburg man".

> *Griffin's death left more than just aching hearts. He also left a lot of work to do, since he ran a flourishing business baling more than 500 acres per year across Sussex County. With his death, Griffin's family would have lost a lot of income, and so the farming community decided to chip in.*

135

"We decided we were going to do it for them", said Jessica Smith. "And then everybody from every direction wanted to bale. They wanted to help. They wanted to do this.

"All farmers came together for one farmer yesterday", Jessica said. "It's great. None of us are family, but when you farm, everyone's a family. It's you know one person is in need and it's kind of like a big family. They're all willing to help".

Highlight the parts of this story that connect to descriptors of the harvest season and to other parts of the everyday story and biblical story. Then, use the story linking process to continue to make connections between all four sections. *If time to explore the questions below, do so in small groups. If no time remains, encourage participants to explore these questions, write down their thoughts, and bring them to the next session.*

What message seems to emerge for your individual life and for the life of your congregation? What is a way God calls us to live faithfully in the harvest season?

Gleanings from Lesson Five

During the week, it is helpful to go back and review the lesson. It is not required but sometimes sitting with scripture and stories can help us grow spiritually. If there are any questions you didn't answer during the session, now may be a time to sit with the question to seek the answer that comes to you.

You are encouraged to journal, writing down your thoughts or stories that come to mind, or to write prayers specific to the season you just discussed. Either way, spend some time re-visiting this season as a personal reflection for yourself and your church.

Day One: What was the most important thing I learned about myself and the harvest season?

Day Two: What was the most important thing I learned about my church and the harvest season?

Day Three: What do I see as the greatest challenge of the harvest season?

Day Four: What do I see as the greatest opportunity in the harvest season?

Day Five: What words or prayer would you like to say to

God about the harvest season? What questions do you have?

What praises do you have?

Session 6: Moving Forward with the End in Mind

Experience

Stephen Covey, author of *The 7 Habits of Highly Effective People*, listed Habit Two as "Begin with the End in Mind". Farmers have employed this habit long before Covey's 1989 book. The harvest that one seeks has to be in one's mind before buying seed, tilling the ground, or even planning for the care of the growing plant. When undertaking an endeavor, there must be a plan—even if it gets changed along the way—to reach a desired result.

Questions to consider:

What do you think about the following quote by Doe Zantamata? "What you see depends on how you see the world: to most people this is just dirt; to a farmer, it is potential".

What kind of seeds do we "plant" in our lives? What end result do we hope for? At our church, how do we plan with "the end in mind" when it comes to being God's farm?

Explore

We are God's farm for a purpose, to yield a harvest for the kingdom. According to author Peter Walker in his book, *The Bible and the Land: An Encounter,* he writes,

> In the Christological logic of Paul the land (like the law), particular and provision have become irrelevant. The land for him has been "christified". It is not the Promised Land that became his "inheritance" but the Living Lord, in whom was a new creation...to be in Christ...has replaced being in the land as the ideal life... for the promised land signifies the Kingdom of God.

How do the following scriptures inform us and our churches to be God's farm for a purpose? Galatians 6:7–10; 2 Corinthians 5:17; Colossians 3:23–24. What do you see as the purpose for your church? What are you called to do with the "land" God has given you?

Engage

In Kathleen Norris' book, *Dakota: A Spiritual Geography*, she tells of Hope Presbyterian church as located by itself in the South Dakota prairie. The church is the neighborhood church that understands the power of community and working together for the good of God. Norris describes it in the following way:

> *Hope's members take seriously their responsibility as members of the world's diverse and largely poor human race...in recent hard times, while Hope's membership declined by nearly half, the amount the church donates for mission has increased every year. It now ranks near the top in per capita giving among Presbyterian churches in the state of South Dakota.*
>
> *Hope is where I realized how much the members of a rural church actually work as well as worship together. They live supporting each other...it's a power derived from smallness and lack of power, a concept the apostle Paul would appreciate...*
>
> *He (one pastor) said, "City people want hymns that reassure them that God is at work in the world, but*

141

the people in the western Dakotas take that for grant-ed". (pp.166–168)

Small and rural churches are as important as the small farms that are scattered across our county. While these churches may seem insignificant to the twenty-first century culture around us, God assures us we are called according to God's purpose and plan. We are told in Zechariah 4:10a () "Do not despise these small beginnings, for the Lord rejoices to see the work begin. . «. How do you hear hope for your life and your congregation in Norris' experience?

Extend

Ellen F. Davis writes the following in "Scripture, Culture, and Agriculture":

> *A contemporary prayer delineates accurately the biblical understanding that our intended service to the land is a holy obligation precisely because it is part of our service to God: Give us all a reverence for the earth as your own creation, that we may use its resources rightly in the service of others and to your honor and glory... (30)*

Throughout this study, we have looked at our

connection to the land and what it looks like to live in the four spiritual seasons. Seasons are cyclical; all seasons come and go in a cycle. We also experience seasonal cycles in the life of our church based on the church year, based on the calendar year, and based spiritually on our growth as God's farm. We are never meant to stay stuck in one season but to continuously be growing and dying to self so we can grow even more. We must remember that the harvest for us is not about building kingdoms or stockpiles for ourselves but building the kingdom of God now and to come.

With that in mind, discuss and answer the following questions:

What season are you currently experiencing in your life? Is it different that at the beginning of this study?

What season is your congregation currently experiencing? Is it the same or different than what you thought at the beginning of this study?

What message has God given you in how to live faithfully in this season?

Within your current season, how can you connect with your community and share the Good News?

What questions do you still have about being faithful as God's farm?

Gleanings from Lesson Six

During the week, it is helpful to go back and review the lesson. It is not required but sometimes sitting with scripture and stories can help us grow spiritually.

Sit quietly for one minute with one thought, "We are God's church". After that time, what images come into your mind? What words, scriptures or songs come to mind? What does God want you to know about being God's farm?

Take at least five minutes to sit with these thoughts, then offer a prayer to God, thanking Him for His faithfulness and provision in each season.

ENDNOTES

Chapter One

1 Witness Lee, *"Fulfillment of God's Purpose by the Growth of Christ in Us.* (Anaheim, CA: Living Stream Ministry Publishing, 1965) 54.

2 James Weldon Johnson, "The Creation", *God's Trombones: Severn Negro Sermons in Verse,* (New York: Penguin Books, 2008) 17.

3 Dietrich Bonhoeffer, *Creation and Fall* (Minneapolis, MN: Fortress Press, 2007) 76.

4 Bonhoeffer, *Creation and Fall,* 77.

5 Ellen Davis, *Scripture, Culture and Agriculture: An Agrarian Reading of the Bible* (New York: Cambridge University Press, 2009) 29.

6 Walter Bruggeman, *The Land: Place as Gift, Promise, and Challenge in Biblical Faith* (Minneapolis, MN: Fortress Press, 2002) xiii.

7 Bruggeman, *The Land,* 62.

8 Bruggeman, *The Land,* 168.

9 Lisa Loden, Peter Walker, and Michael Wood, ed., *The Bible and the Land: An Encounter: Different Views: Christian Arab Palestinian, Israeli Messianic Jew, Western Christian* (Jerusalem: Musalaha, 2000) 133-134.

10 Hymn of Promise, Accessed 12/30/2016, http://www.hymntime.com/tch/htm/h/y/m/hymnprom.htm.

11 T.S. Eliot, "East Coker" from The Four Quartets poems, Accessed 2/2/2018, http://oedipa.tripod.com/eliot-2.html ,

12 Natalie Sleeth, Hymn of Promise", The United Methodist Hymnal (Nashville, TN: The United Methodist Publishing House, 1989) 707.

13 Thurman, Howard, *Deep is the Hunger* (New York: Harper and Row, 1951) 89-90.

14 Philip Sheldrake, *Spirituality: A Brief History.* (West Sussex, UK: Wiley-Blackwell, 2013) 167.

15 Frederick Norwood, *The Story of American Methodism.*

(Nashville, TN: Abingdon Press, 1974) 159-160.
16 Aaron Earls. "Facts & Trends: majority of American Churches fall below 100 in worship". Accessed 2/12/2018, https://factsandtrends.net/2016/02/24/majority-of-american-churches-fall-below-100-in-worship-attendance/
17 Walter Bruggeman. *The Land: Place as Gift, Promise, and Challenge in Biblical Faith.* (Minneapolis, MN: Fortress Press. 2002.) xxii.
18 Bruggeman, *The Land,* 1.
19 Bruggeman. *The Land,* 4.
20 Bruggeman. *The Land,* 5.
21 Bruggeman. *The Land,* 173.
22 Bruggeman. *The Land* 202.
23 Kathleen Norris. *Dakota: A Spiritual Geography,* (New York: First Mariner Books, 2001.) 37.
24 Norris, *Dakota,* 167-168.
25 Norris, *Dakota,* 169.
26 Norris, *Dakota,* 169-170.
27 Norris, *Dakota,* 164.
28 Norris, *Dakota,* 164.
29 Bruggeman, *The Land,* 15-16.
30 Jurgen Moltmann. *God in Creation* (Minneapolis, MN: Fortress Press, 1993) 51.
31 Moltmann, *God in Creation.,* 186.
32 Diana Butler Bass, *Grounded: Finding God in the World – A Spiritual Revolution* (New York: HarperOne, 2015) 26.
33 Butler Bass, *Grounded,* 50.
34 Butler Bass, *Grounded,* 58.
35 Butler Bass, *Grounded,* 58.
36 Ellen Davis, Scripture, *Culture and Agriculture: An Agrarian Reading of the Bible.* (New York: Cambridge University Press, 2009) 2.
37 Davis, *Scripture, Culture and Agriculture,* 8.
38 Davis, *Scripture, Culture and Agriculture,* 133
39 Davis, *Scripture, Culture and Agriculture* ,38.
40 Ernest Kurtz and Katherine Ketcham, *The Spirituality of*

Imperfection: Storytelling and the Search for Meaning (New York: Bantam Books, 1992) 42.
41 Kurtz, *The Spirituality of Imperfection*, 19.
42 Howard Thurman, *Disciplines of the Spirit.* (Richmond, IN: Friends United Press, 1963) 21.
43 Wendell Berry",Standing By Words", (Berkley: Counterpoint, 2008) 72.
44 Berry, "Standing By Words", 73.
45 Berry, "Standing By Words", 2.
46 Daniel J. Stulac, "A Gospel of the Ground", *Plough Quarterly* (Walden, NY: Plough Publishing House, Spring 2015) 28.
47 Stulac, "A Gospel of the Ground", 27.
48 Janet Raloff. "Dirt is not Soil"., Accessed 10/26/2018. https://www.sciencenews.org/blog/science-public/dirt-not-soil.
Chapter Two
49 U. S. Department of Agriculture Economic Research Services Rural Classification. Accessed 5/15/2018, http://www.ers.usda.gov/topics/rural-economy-population/rural-classifications/what is rural.aspx.
50 Lyle E. Schaller, *Small Congregation, Big Potential: Ministry in the Small Membership Church* (Nashville, TN: Abingdon Press, 2003) 26.
51 Schaller, *Small Congregation, Big Potential: Ministry in the Small Membership Church*, 24.
52 Heather Hahn, "Places of the heart: Rural church at crossroads", Accessed 10/9/2017, http://www.umc.org/news-and-media/places-of-the-heart-rural-church-at-crossroads-page-2.
53 Hahn, "Places of the heart"
54 "Delaware Agricultural Statistics", www.nass.usda.gov/Statistics_by_State/Delaware, Accessed May 1, 2018
55 Bailey, L.H., *The Holy Earth*, (Michigan, Michigan State University Press: 2008) 24.
56 Bailey, *The Holy Earth*, 26.
57 Masanobu Fukuoka, *The One-Straw Revolution* (New

York: New York Review Book, 1978) 21.

58 Fukuoka, *The One-Straw Revolution*,113.

59 Lewis A. Parks, *Preaching in the Small Membership Church* (Nashville, TN: Abingdon Press, 2009) 15.

60 Golemon, Larry A. Ed., *Finding Our Story: Narrative Leadership and Congregational Change* (New York: The Alban Institute, 2010) 11.

61 Goleman, *Finding Our Story*, 17.

62 Mann, Alice, "Place-Based Narratives: An entry point for ministry to the soul of a community", *Finding Our Story: Narrative Leadership and Congregational Change* (New York: The Alban Institute, 2010) 59.

63 Mann, *Finding Our Story*, 74-75.

64 Mann, *Finding Our Story*, 81.

65 Mann, *Finding Our Story*, 81.

66 Tom Berlin and Lovett H. Weems, Jr. *High Yield: Seven Disciplines of the Fruitful Leader*. (Nashville, TN: Abingdon Press. 2014) 19

67 Ibid. 19.

68 Lewis Parks. *Small on Purpose: Life in a Significant Church.* (Nashville: Abingdon Press. 2017) 60.

69 Parks, *Small on Purpose*, 42.

70 Pappas, Anthony G., *Entering the World of the Small Church* (New York: Alban Institute, 2000) 5.

71 Pappas, *Entering the World*.

72 Sanders, Noah, *Born-Again Dirt: Farming to the Glory of God,* (Rora Valley Publishing, 2012) 17-18.

73 Sanders, *Born-Again Dirt*, 47.

74 Masanobu Fukuoka, *The One Straw Revolution,* Rodale Press,1978, xiv.

75 Wendell Berry, *The Unsettling of America: Culture and Agriculture* (Counterpoint, 1977).

Chapter Three

76 Howard Thurman, *Deep is the Hunger* (Friends United Press, 1951) 48.

77 Thurman, *Deep is the Hunger*, 49.

78 Anne E. Streaty Wimberly, *Soul Stories: African American Christian Education*, (Nashville, TN: Abingdon Press, 2005), 26.

79 Larry A. Golemon, Ed., *Finding Our Story: Narrative Leadership and Congregational Change*, (New York: The Alban Institute, 2010), 5.

80 Appendix .

81 Sensing, *Qualitative Research*, 158.

82 FFA History, Accessed May 21, 2018, https://www.ffa.org/about/what-is-ffa/ffa-history.

Chapter Six

83 "Great is Thy Faithfulness", The United Methodist Hymnal (Nashville, TN: The United Methodist Publishing House, 1989) 140.

84 FFA Creed, Accessed May 21, 2018, https://www.ffa.org/creed.

85 Thom Rainer. Why Smaller Churches are Making a Comeback. Accessed 9/1/2019,https://thomrainer.com/2019/07/why-smaller-churches-are-making-a-comeback/.

_____

Session 1
Ellen Davis, *Scripture, Culture and Agriculture, 29*
Witness Lee, *"Fulfillment of God's Purpose by the Growth of Christ in Us. (Anaheim, CA: Living Stream Ministry Publishing, 1965) 54*

_____

Session 2
Janet Peters. "The Fallow Field: the Virtue of Doing Nothing". *Science and Health* (blog). https://spiritualityhealth.com/blogs/downward-blog-a-life-in-yoga/2014/03/06/jc-peters-fallow-field-virtue-doing-nothing. Accessed 1/2/2017.

Session 3
Christine Hoover. "Three Lessons from the Farmer about Faith". (http://www.desiringgod.org/articles/three-lessons-from-the-farmer-about-faith.) Accessed 2/4/2017.

Session 5
"Farming Community Rallies Behind Killed Parsonsburg
Man. https:// http://www.wboc.com/story/32420785/farm-
ing-community-rallies-behind-killed-parsonsburg-man.
Accessed 7/16/2016.

Session 6
Kathleen Norris. *Dakota: A Spiritual Geography*, (New York:
First Mariner Books, 2001.) 166-168.

Bibliography

Adeyemo, Tokunboh. *Africa Bible Commentary*, Grand Rapids. Zondervan. 2006.

Bailey, L.H.. The Holy Earth. Michigan State University-Press. 2008.24, 26

Bartlett, David and Barbara Brown Taylor, ed. *Feasting on the Word, Year A, Vol. 1*. Louisville. Westminster John Knox Press, 2010.

Bass, Diana Butler. *Grounded: Finding God in the World – A Spiritual Revolution*. New York. HarperOne, 2015.

Berlin, Tom and Lovett H. Weems, Jr. *High Yield: Seven Disciplines of the Fruitful Leader*. Nashville: Abingdon Press. 2014.

Berry, Wendell. "Standing By Words". Berkley: Counterpoint, 2008.

Berry, Wendell. *The Mad Farmer Poems*. Berkeley: Counterpoint, 2013.

Berry, Wendell, *The Unsettling of America: Culture and Agriculture*. Counterpoint, 1977.

Bonheoffer, Dietrich. *Creation and Fall*. Minneapolis: Fortress Press, 2007.

Bruggeman, Walter. *The Land: Place as Gift, Promise, and Challenge in Biblical Faith*. Minneapolis: Fortress Press. 2002.

"Church Health Survey Results Analysis Packet for Wesley United Methodist Church, Georgetown, DE from the Lawless Group". Received by Wesley UMC Church Council, October, 2016.

"Commentary on 1 Corinthians 3:1–9". https://www.workingpreacher.org/preaching.aspx? commentary_id=1950 Accessed 6/19/2016.

Covey, Steven. *The 7 Habits of Highly Effective People*. New York: Simon and Shuster, 1989.

Davis, Ellen. *Scripture, Culture and Agriculture: An Agrarian Reading of the Bible*. New York: Cambridge University Press, 2009.

"Delaware Agricultural Statistics". www.nass.usda.gov/ Statistics_by_State/Delaware. Accessed May 1, 2018.

The Discipleship Study Bible, NRSV, Louisville: Westminister John Knox Press, 2008

Eliot, T.S.. "East Coker" from The Four Quartets poems. http://oedipa.tripod.com/eliot-2.html, Accessed 2/2/2018.

Future Farmers of America. http://www.ffa.org/about/whatt-is-ffa/ffa-history. Accessed May 21, 2018.

Fukuoka, Masanobu. *The One-Straw Revolution*. New York: New York Review Book. 1978.

Golemon, Larry A., ed. *Finding Our Story: Narrative Leadership and Congregational Change*. New York: The Alban Institute, 2010.

Hahn, Heather. "Places of the heart: Rural church at crossroads".http://www.umc.org/news-and-media/places-of-the-heart-rural-church-at-crossroads, Accessed 10/9/2017.

Hamilton-Poore, Sam. *Earth Gospel*. Nashville: Upper Room Books, 2008.

Hauerwas, Stanley and L. Gregory Jones, ed. *Why narrative? Readings in narrative theology*. Eugene, Oregon: Wipf and Stock Publisher, 1997.

"Inheritance", Bakers Evangelical Dictionary of Bible Theology. http://www.biblestudytools.com/ dictionaries/ bakers-evangelical-dictionary/.html, Accessed 6/20/2016.

Johnson, James Weldon. "The Creation". *God's Trombones: Seven Negro Sermons in Verse*. New York: Penguin Books, 2008.

Kurtz, Ernest and Katherine Ketcham. *The Spirituality of Imperfection: Storytelling and the Search for Meaning*. New York: Bantam Books, 1992.

Lacroix, Len and Jennifer Lacriox. "The Beauty of Brokenness", *Seeking the Lord* (blog), http://len-seekingthelord.logspot.com/2011/07/beauty-of-brokenness.html. Accessed   6/5/2016

Lee, Witness. *"Fulfillment of God's Purpose by the Growth of Christ in Us.* Anaheim, CA: Living Stream Ministry Publishing, 1965.

Lisa Loden, Peter Walker, and Michael Wood. ed., *The Bible and the Land: An Encounter: Different Views: Christian Arab Palestinian, Israeli Messianic Jew, Western Christian.*   Jerusalem: Musalaha, 2000.

Mann, Alice. "Place-Based Narratives: An entry point for ministry to the soul of a community".

Finding Our Story: Narrative Leadership and Congregational Change. Herndon, VA: The Alban Institute, 2010.

Moltmann, Jurgen. *God in Creation.* Minneapolis, MN: Fortress Press, 1993.

Morgan, Elisa. *The Orchard: A parable*. Grand Rapids, MI: Revell, 2006.

Moschella, Mary Clark. "Enlivening Local Stories through Pastoral Ethnography". *Teaching Our Story: Narrative Leadership and Congregational Change.* Herndon, VA: The Alban   Institute, 2010.

Nee, Watchman. *The Release of the Spirit.* New York: Christian Fellowship Publishers, 2014.

Norris, Kathleen. *"Dakota: A Spiritual Geography".* New York: First Mariner Books, 2001.

Norwood, Frederick. *The Story of American Methodism.* Nashville, TN: Abingdon Press, 1974.

Nouwen, Henri. *Spiritual Formation: Following the Movements of the Spirit.* New York: HarperOne, 2010.

"Number of local churches as distributed by average attendance at the principle weekly worship service and by annual conference". http://www.gcfa.org/data-services-statistics Accessed 10/2/17

Pappas, Anthony G. *Entering the World of the Small Church.* Herndon, VA: Alban Institute, 2000.

Parks, Lewis A. *Preaching in the Small Membership Church.* Nashville: Abingdon Press. 2009.

Parks, Lewis A. *Small on Purpose: Life in a Significant Church.* Nashville Abingdon Press, 2017.

Peters, Janet. "The Fallow Field: the Virtue of Doing Nothing". *Science and Health* (blog). https://spiritualityhealth.com/blogs/downward-blog-a-life-in-yoga/2014/03/06/jc-peters-fallow-field-virtue-doing-nothing. Accessed 1/2/2017.

Raloff, Janet. "Dirt is not Soil". https://www.sciencenews.org/blog/science-public/dirt-not-soil, Accessed 10/26/2018.

Sa, Kyung-Hee. "Dover District Churches Journal Statistics from 2012, 2013, 2014. Peninsula Delaware Conference of The United Methodist Church". Report presented at Dover   District clergy meeting January 2016.

Robinson, Robert H. and Daniel G. Coston Jr. *Old Country Churches of Sussex County, DE.* Georgetown, DE: Sussex Prints. 1976.

"Rural Life Sunday". https://www.umcdiscipleship.org/resources/rural-life-sunday. Accessed 4/1/2018.

Sanders, Noah. *Born-Again Dirt: Farming to the Glory of God.* Rora Valley Publishing. 2012.

Lyle E. Schaller. *Small Congregation, Big Potential: Ministry in the Small Membership Church.* Nashville: Abingdon Press, 2003.

Tim Sensing, *Qualitative Research: A Multi-methods Approach to Projects for Doctor of Ministry Theses.* Eugene, OR: Wipf and Stock, 2011.

Sheldrake, Philip. *Spirituality: A Brief History.* West Sussex, UK: Wiley-Blackwell. 2013.

Stulac, Daniel J. "A Gospel of the Ground". *Plough Quarterly.* Walden, NY: Plough Publishing House. Spring 2015.

The United Methodist Hymnal. Nashville, TN: The United Methodist Publishing House, 1989

Thomas, Robert B. *The Old Farmer's Almanac 2018.* Dublin, NH: Yankee Publishing Incorporated, 2017.

Thurman, Howard. *Deep is the Hunger.* New York: Harper and Row. 1951.48, 49

Howard Thurman, *Disciplines of the Spirit* (Richmond, IN: Friends United Press, 1963) 21.

"Times and Seasons of the Agricultural Year". https:// www.churchofengland.org/ prayer-and-worship/ worship-texts-and-resources/common-worship/ churches-year/ times-and-seasons/agricultural-year Accessed 4/1/2018.

U. S. Department of Agriculture Economic Research Services Rural Classification. http://www.ers.usda.gov/topics/ rural-economy-population/rural-classifications/what is rural.aspx . Accessed 5/15/2018

Vang, Preben. *Teach the Text Commentary Series: 1 Corinthians.* Grand Rapids, MI. Baker Books. 2014.

Williams, William H. *A History of Wesley U.M. Church: Georgetown 1779–1978.* Georgetown, DE: The Countian Press. 1978.

Wimberly, Anne E. Streaty. *Soul Stories: African American Christian Education.* Nashville: Abingdon Press. 2005.

ABOUT THE AUTHOR

Reverend Rebecca "Becky" Kelly Collison, an ordained Methodist pastor, holds a bachelor's degree in special education from University of Maryland Eastern Shore, a master's in education from Wilmington (College) University, and a master's of divinity and a doctorate of ministry, both from Wesley Theological Seminary in Washington, DC.

When not at the parsonage of her current pastoral appointment, she lives with her husband Glenn on the corner of the family farm in Harrington, Delaware, and enjoys the company of family, including their six children and seven grandchildren.

REBECCA COLLISON

CPSIA information can be obtained
at www.ICGtesting.com
Printed in the USA
LVHW080742190922
728708LV00008B/342